Planet Earth

RIVERS AND LAKES

Other Publications:

AMERICAN COUNTRY
VOYAGE THROUGH THE UNIVERSE
THE THIRD REICH
THE TIME-LIFE GARDENER'S GUIDE
MYSTERIES OF THE UNKNOWN
TIME FRAME
FIX IT YOURSELF
FITNESS, HEALTH & NUTRITION
SUCCESSFUL PARENTING
HEALTHY HOME COOKING
UNDERSTANDING COMPUTERS
LIBRARY OF NATIONS
THE ENCHANTED WORLD
THE KODAK LIBRARY OF CREATIVE PHOTOGRAPHY
GREAT MEALS IN MINUTES
THE CIVIL WAR
COLLECTOR'S LIBRARY OF THE CIVIL WAR
THE EPIC OF FLIGHT
THE GOOD COOK
WORLD WAR II
HOME REPAIR AND IMPROVEMENT
THE OLD WEST

For information on and a full description of any of
the Time-Life Books series listed above, please call
1-800-621-7026 or write:
    Reader Information
    Time-Life Customer Service
    P.O. Box C-32068
    Richmond, Virginia 23261-2068

This volume is one of a series that examines the
wonders of the planet earth, from its landforms,
seas and atmosphere to its place in the cosmos.

Cover
Spring runoff cascades into the placid waters of
Austria's Gosau Lake, part of a system of
mountain streams and glacial lakes that drains
into tributaries of the Danube River.

Planet Earth

RIVERS AND LAKES

By Laurence Pringle
and The Editors of Time-Life Books

Time-Life Books, Alexandria, Virginia

PLANET EARTH

SERIES DIRECTOR: Gerald Simons
Designer: Raymond Ripper
Series Coordinator: Caroline A. Boubin

Editorial Staff for *Rivers and Lakes*
Associate Editor: Jean B. Crawford (pictures)
Text Editor: Thomas H. Flaherty Jr.
Staff Writer: Rita Thievon Mullin
Researchers: Susan S. Blair, Norma Kennedy
(principals), Patti H. Cass
Assistant Designer: Cynthia T. Richardson
Copy Coordinators: Kelly Banks, Elizabeth Graham
Picture Coordinator: Renée DeSandies
Special Contributors: Ronald H. Bailey,
Charles C. Smith (text)

Editorial Operations
Copy Chief: Diane Ullius
Editorial Operations Manager: Caroline A. Boubin
Production: Celia Beattie
Quality Control: James J. Cox (director)
Library: Louise D. Forstall

Correspondents: Elisabeth Kraemer-Singh (Bonn);
Maria Vincenza Aloisi (Paris); Ann Natanson
(Rome). Valuable assistance was also provided by:
Janny Hovinga, Wibo van de Linde (Amsterdam);
Robert Gilmore, Di Webster (Auckland); Angelika
Lemmer (Bonn); Robert Kroon (Geneva); Elizabeth
Heasman (London); John Dunn (Melbourne); Felix
Rosenthal (Moscow); Christina Lieberman (New
York); Dag Christensen (Oslo); Patricia Robb, Gavin
Scott (Rio); Ann Wise (Rome); Dick Berry
(Tokyo); Traudl Lessing (Vienna).

Library of Congress Cataloguing in Publication Data
Pringle, Laurence P.
    Rivers and lakes.
    (Planet earth)
    Bibliography: p.
    Includes index.
    1. Rivers.   2. Lakes.   3. Freshwater biology.
I. Time-Life Books.   II. Title.   III. Series.
GB1205.P75 1985   551.48   84-24463
ISBN 0-8094-4508-5
ISBN 0-8094-4509-3 (lib. bdg.)

THE AUTHOR
Laurence Pringle has written more than 40
books on biological and environmental subjects.
Among these are *Wild River,* a book about the
ecology and hydrology of North American wilderness rivers, and *Water,* an examination of the
water crisis threatening the United States. He
studied wildlife conservation at Cornell University and received the National Wildlife Feder-
ation's Special Conservation Award in 1978.

THE CONSULTANT
Robert C. Averett is regional research hydrologist for the U.S. Department of the Interior's
Geological Survey in Denver, Colorado. Author
of more than 50 scientific papers, he has done
research work on a number of rivers and lakes in
the Western and Central United States and has
been associated with similar studies in Canada.

CONTENTS

FROM THE SOURCE TO THE SEA

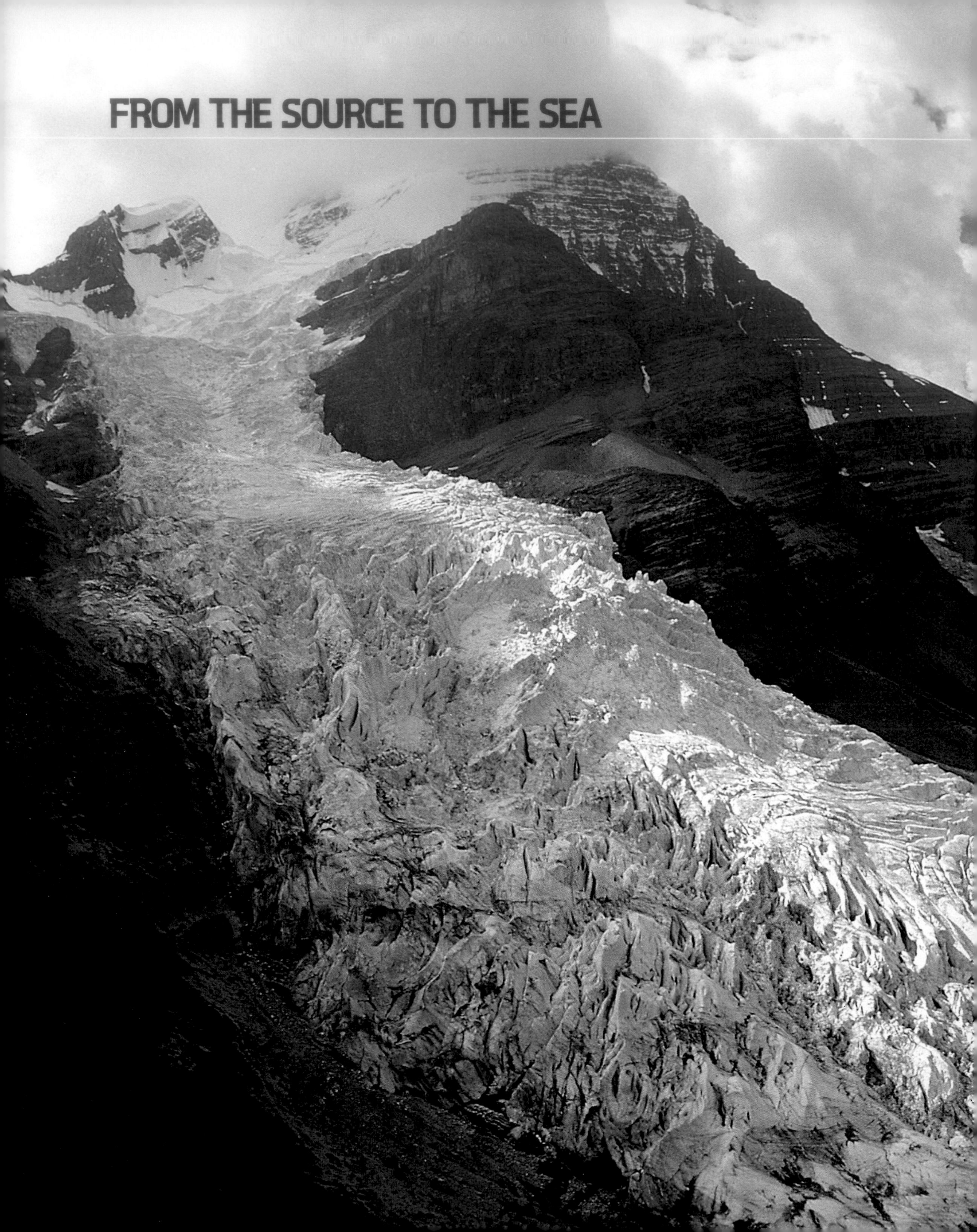

Berg Lake, source of the Robson River, nestles in the Canadian Rockies. The glacier at left sometimes calves icebergs, which gave the lake its name.

Wreathed in mist, the Li River flows past clusters of toothlike hills in central China. After 250 miles, the Li dead-ends in Tungting Lake.

Totem Lake, part of a system that feeds the Columbia River, mirrors its waterside larches and a lofty peak in British Columbia's Purcell Mountains.

The Iguassú River breaks into waterfalls along a two-and-one-half-mile crest line, plunging 200 feet into a narrow gorge on the Brazil-Argentina border.

Meandering southward through its swampy delta, the Atchafalaya River in Louisiana empties into a bay *(top)* adjoining the Gulf of Mexico.

EXPLORING INLAND WATERS

In spite of its reputation for sedate conformity, Victorian England harbored a fair number of footloose romantics. Fearless, aggressive men, they pushed to the far ends of the globe, exploring for the sheer joy of adventure and to expand the body of common knowledge. Several of them chose to seek the source of the Nile, and in that effort they carried their enthusiasm to reckless extremes.

In the 1850s the Nile was a half-told tale. The eastern branch of the upper river, fancifully called the Blue Nile, rises in the southeast end of Lake Tana, on a high plateau in Ethiopia. That much had been discovered in 1615 by a peripatetic Portuguese priest named Pedro Paez. But the western branch of the upper river, the White Nile, was virtually unknown until it joined the Blue Nile at the city of Khartoum, more than 1,000 miles south of the Mediterranean Sea. The ultimate source of the White Nile was one of the world's great remaining geographic mysteries.

In 1857 two daring Britishers joined forces to solve the mystery. They made an unlikely team. Richard Francis Burton, already a famed adventurer at the age of 36, was scholarly and melancholic, with "the brow of a god," wrote an acquaintance, "and the jaw of a devil." John Hanning Speke, six years Burton's junior and a rank neophyte at exploration, was vigorous, ambitious and a skilled hunter of big game.

Mounting an expedition of more than 100 porters, Burton and Speke set out from the Indian Ocean port of Zanzibar. They followed the route inland pioneered by Arab slave traders and soon entered uncharted regions where no Europeans had ever set foot. For eight months they endured tropical heat, debilitating diseases and the constant threat of hostile natives. In the end they made a marvelous discovery: Lake Tanganyika, the world's sixth-largest fresh-water lake. But to the partners' disappointment, the only river they found there flowed south into the lake and hence could not be the White Nile.

While Burton took time to write up his notes, Speke impatiently headed north. In that direction, Speke had heard from an Arab, lay a lake "so broad that you could not see across it and so long that nobody knew its length." Traveling alone, Speke found the lake in less than a month and named it Victoria after Britain's reigning monarch. Lake Victoria straddles the Equator and embraces 26,828 square miles — twice the surface area of its neighbor Tanganyika. It is the earth's second largest fresh-water lake.

Speke was convinced that Victoria was the source of the White Nile. Burton was skeptical; after all, Speke had seen only the lake and not any

In this 18th Century illustration of a Hindu myth, the god Shiva, seated with his wife Parvati on Mount Kailas in the Himalayas, lets the sacred river Ganges flow to earth through his hair. In reality, the source of the Ganges is about 100 miles to the west, where the river emerges from the Gangotri glacier.

link to the Nile. Speke himself realized that the job was not finished; he returned to England to announce his discovery and to raise funds for a second expedition. He and Burton were henceforth irreconcilable rivals.

Speke's new expedition reached the northwest shore of Lake Victoria in 1862 and found a river — obviously the Nile, he thought — pouring northward out of the lake over a great waterfall. "The Nile is settled," Speke cabled London.

But was it? Speke still had failed to follow the river far enough north to prove that it was the White Nile, and he had also failed to exhaust the possibilities of a more distant source. Burton, who had not been offered a place in the expedition, seized upon these discrepancies to lead a vociferous group of anti-Speke theorists. Amid bitter wrangling, Speke and Burton in 1864 agreed to debate before an audience of several hundred eminent geographers and scientists. The confrontation never took place; just before it, Speke was found shot to death. Burton believed that his former partner had committed suicide rather than debate him, but a coroner's jury ruled that Speke had shot himself accidentally while hunting.

Now a new seeker appeared. He was David Livingstone, a gentle British physician and a missionary-explorer who wanted most of all to help end the African slave trade. Like Burton, Livingstone believed that the true source of the White Nile lay well to the southwest of Lake Victoria, and in 1865 he set out to find it. But soon many members of his expedition succumbed to disease and others deserted. The doctor himself fell ill and lost touch with the outside world.

To find Livingstone, a new expedition took the field under the leadership of 30-year-old Henry Morton Stanley, the star correspondent of the *New York Herald,* which had financed the trip to boost circulation. Stanley was an Americanized Britisher; at an early age, he had run away from an English workhouse, crossed the Atlantic as a cabin boy, fought in the Civil War and won fame as a reporter on the Western frontier.

On November 10, 1871, Stanley marched into the town of Ujiji, near Lake Tanganyika. There he saw a frail, white-bearded old man standing in front of a semicircle of Arabs. Stanley took off his hat and made a perfectly normal remark that soon echoed throughout the world as high melodrama: "Dr. Livingstone, I presume?"

The abrasive Stanley and the saintly Livingstone became friends. Two years later, Livingstone died, and Stanley undertook to prove the doctor's theory that the Nile originated southwest of Lake Victoria in a river called the Lualaba. But his explorations soon showed that the Lualaba actually fed Africa's other great river, the Congo (now the Zaire). In fact, he bolstered Speke's claim. By circumnavigating Lake Victoria in 1875, Stanley found that the lake had only one major outlet — presumably the Nile — and one main inlet, a river called the Kagera, flowing in from the southwest.

It remained for other explorers to round out the work of Speke and Burton and Stanley by following the course of the White Nile from Victoria all the way north to its junction with the Blue Nile. This was done before the turn of the 20th Century. Yet even then, something was missing. At first, it appeared that the Kagera River merely emptied into Victoria. But actually the Kagera contributed its flow to the White Nile: It sent a barely perceptible current across the northwestern corner of the lake to the waterfall where the White Nile journeys north.

John Hanning Speke, the British explorer who discovered Lake Victoria in 1858, is portrayed at the northern end of the lake, where Ripon Falls pours into the White Nile. Speke believed that this was the source of the White Nile, but the ultimate source actually lies about 500 miles southwest of this spot.

Not until the 1930s did someone follow this clue to its logical conclusion and wrestle into place one last piece in the puzzle of the river's origins. A lone, impoverished German explorer named Burkhart Waldecker traced the winding Kagera southwest for 250 miles to a mountainside in what is now Berundi. There, only 60 miles from Lake Tanganyika's northern tip, which Burton and Speke had first seen nearly eight decades before, Waldecker came upon 10 tiny springs trickling into a ravine. These are the humble beginnings of the Kagera and of the White Nile.

At that place, more than 4,150 miles from the Mediterranean, Waldecker later erected a 10-foot-high pyramid bearing a bronze plaque inscribed with the Latin *Caput Nili* — Source of the Nile — and a list of all those theorists and explorers who had sought this place over a span of nearly 2,500 years, each contributing an important fragment of the truth.

Why did so many men give so much of their lives and health to find the source of the White Nile? Among their many motives, of course, was the fact that the Nile had nurtured the ancient kingdom of Egypt and thereby had contributed vitally to the development of Western civilization. The river is remarkable still for helping to support a population of more than 59 million Ugandans, Sudanese and Egyptians.

The Nile's importance and historic appeal are examples of the unique contributions made by inland waters to the earth's complex makeup. On every continent, rivers large and small sustain human life. Together with fresh-water lakes they occupy less than 2 per cent of the earth's surface, but they furnish food, slake thirst, carry commerce, irrigate farms, cool machinery, flush away industrial and domestic wastes, generate electrical power and provide recreation for untold millions of people.

Beyond providing these practical benefits, inland waters do something more. They speak to the human spirit, offering beauty and inviting adventure. As novelist H. E. Bates once wrote: "Water has some kind of powerful mystery about it. Still waters, moving waters, dark waters; the words themselves have a mysterious, almost dying fall."

Inland waters — both rivers and lakes — are linked symbiotically in fact as in poetry. For all the differences between rivers and lakes — in size, shape, age, geological origin and, above all, in the fact that rivers flow while most lakes move only imperceptibly — they typically depend on each other. Rivers often give birth to lakes and may eventually kill their creations by filling them with sediments. Lakes and their smaller versions, ponds, may themselves serve as sources of rivers.

But on a more fundamental level, rivers and lakes are joined in the worldwide system from which both ultimately receive their waters — the hydrologic cycle. The earth's water is in a constant state of circulation powered by the heat of the sun and the pull of gravity. Water evaporates, and as it rises in the atmosphere, this water vapor cools and collects into clouds. Then, at the proper conditions of temperature and moisture content, water vapor condenses and returns to earth as rain and snow for temporary storage in rivers, lakes and oceans, in polar icecaps and glaciers, and under the ground.

This endless cycle of circulation was only dimly understood by early scholars. Greek and Roman thinkers, in pondering the ultimate sources of rivers, envisioned a vast subterranean plumbing system. They believed that all rivers were fed by large springs, which in turn flowed from underground rivers or lakes that linked up to the distant oceans — the salt water somehow being purified in its long journey.

Various versions of this misconception persisted until the 17th Century, in part because precipitation alone did not seem sufficient to account for the flow of large rivers. Then in 1674, the French scientist Claude Perrault conducted a simple study. He actually measured the annual precipitation that fell in the basin of the upper Seine and compared it with the estimated amount of water flowing in the river. He found that the precipitation added up to six times the amount of water in the Seine, more than enough to account for the river's flow.

A few years later, Perrault's countryman Edmé Mariotte established the existence of another stage in the hydrologic cycle. Working in a cellar at the Paris Observatory, Mariotte noticed that the amount of water leaking in varied with the amount of rainfall. He observed a similar phenomenon at springs: The more it rained, the greater the flow issuing from the ground. He concluded that rainfall fed springs — and leaky basements — by infiltrating the ground and eventually returning to the surface.

A contemporary of these two French scientists, the English astronomer

In this 15th Century copy of a map first drawn around 150 A.D. by Ptolemy, the Nile's sources and course are depicted with surprising accuracy for an age when geographic knowledge and mapmaking were still in their infancy. Ptolemy, a Greek scholar living in Egypt, used merchants' reports as the basis for the map and for his conclusion that one of the Nile's sources flowed from the "Mountains of the Moon," the range now known as the Ruwenzori.

Edmund Halley, helped balance out the equation by demonstrating the role of evaporation in the cycle. Using a small pan of water placed over a bed of hot coals, he calculated the rate of evaporation at a temperature approximating that of "our hottest summers." He then applied this rate to the entire Mediterranean Sea. His estimate of total annual evaporation from that body of water turned out to be amazingly accurate. More important, it just about balanced his estimate of the volume of water pouring into the Mediterranean from rivers every year.

Modern scientists, building on the work of these 17th Century pioneers, estimate that the planet contains 326 million cubic miles of water. At any given time, slightly more than 97 per cent of the total resides in the oceans. A little more than 2 per cent is frozen in icecaps and glaciers. Less than 1 per cent remains for rivers and lakes, underground water and water vapor in the atmosphere. Lakes hold only .017 per cent of all the water, rivers a mere .0001 per cent.

Rivers and lakes receive their waters from any of four different stages of the hydrologic cycle. One source is rain and snow falling directly upon their surfaces. Though this input is minute for most rivers, it can be major for lakes with immense surface areas. Lake Victoria, for one, receives more than 70 per cent of its total supply from rainfall. Precipitation temporarily stored in glaciers also nourishes many inland waters. Perhaps the best known example is the Rhine River, which is fed by meltwater from glaciers in the Swiss Alps.

A third source for rivers and lakes is the vital underground connection, subsurface water. Groundwater represents an enormous reservoir of more than two million cubic miles of water — approximately 37 times the total contained in rivers and lakes. As much as 30 per cent of the volume of rivers and lakes reaches them from underground sources. It has been estimated that groundwater accounts for fully half of the flow of North America's Mississippi.

Precipitation seeps into the ground through a combination of capillary action and the tug of gravity. A tiny fraction of the water is retained by the upper layer of soil and by the root systems of plants. Most of the precipitation drains downward until it is stopped by an underlying layer of bedrock that is watertight. This groundwater accumulates, gradually filling all the openings and cracks in the soil and permeable rock. The top of the underground zone that becomes fully saturated is the water table.

The depth of the water table beneath the earth's surface varies with precipitation and climate. It may range from only a few feet below the ground in humid regions to hundreds or even thousands of feet down in desert areas. The water table is not always flat, as the name implies, but it roughly parallels the surface. Like the overlying terrain, the subsurface layers of water-bearing rock have been warped and folded by movements in the earth's crust. Thus, the contours of the water table tend to rise and fall with the surface topography.

Any water-bearing layer of rock such as sandstone, limestone or gravel is called an aquifer. These underground reservoirs underlie the land everywhere, from frozen Arctic tundra to deserts, where heat and evaporation prevent the formation of permanent rivers or lakes. Typically local in extent, aquifers nevertheless may underlie entire regions. In the United

All through the earth's long history, the same water has been used and reused, frozen, melted, evaporated, condensed and moved from place to place. Each molecule of water passes through every stage and state in the hydrologic cycle.

Water is a liquid whose oxygen atoms are weakly bonded together by hydrogen atoms. The bonds are continually breaking and re-forming, giving liquid water its characteristic properties. When a hydrogen bond is broken by heat, individual molecules evaporate from the surface of the liquid crystal. Water can evaporate from oceans, lakes and rivers, or from the land, where some moisture always stays near the surface, clinging to soil particles. When water absorb-

ed from the soil by roots evaporates through plant surfaces, the process is called transpiration.

As molecules of water vapor lose heat, they begin to condense, re-forming intermolecular hydrogen bonds and clumping together in droplets. Clouds — huge accumulations of droplets — dump liquid or frozen precipitation to the earth, where much of it is locked up in glaciers and icecaps. Seasonal melting liquefies ice and snow, and gravity pulls runoff down slopes, where some soaks into the soil, nourishing plants and replenishing the groundwater. Some of the runoff flows into streams, lakes and oceans, from which water-vapor molecules rise as the cycle goes on.

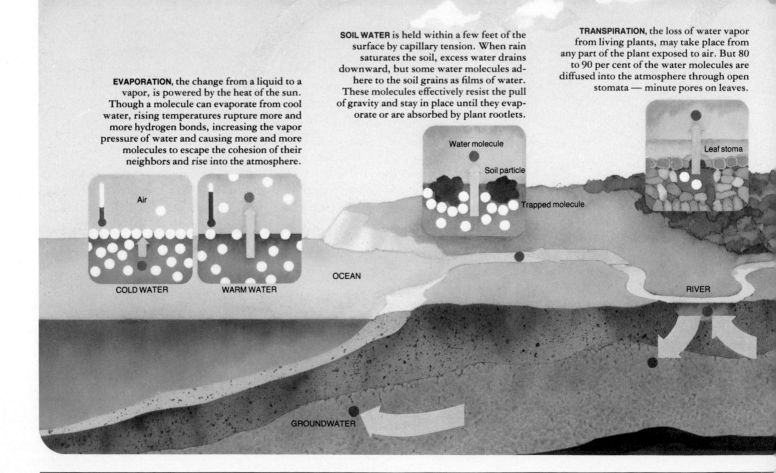

EVAPORATION, the change from a liquid to a vapor, is powered by the heat of the sun. Though a molecule can evaporate from cool water, rising temperatures rupture more and more hydrogen bonds, increasing the vapor pressure of water and causing more and more molecules to escape the cohesion of their neighbors and rise into the atmosphere.

Air

COLD WATER   WARM WATER

SOIL WATER is held within a few feet of the surface by capillary tension. When rain saturates the soil, excess water drains downward, but some water molecules adhere to the soil grains as films of water. These molecules effectively resist the pull of gravity and stay in place until they evaporate or are absorbed by plant rootlets.

Water molecule

Soil particle

Trapped molecule

TRANSPIRATION, the loss of water vapor from living plants, may take place from any part of the plant exposed to air. But 80 to 90 per cent of the water molecules are diffused into the atmosphere through open stomata — minute pores on leaves.

Leaf stoma

OCEAN

RIVER

GROUNDWATER

SNOW forms when water molecules condense on a nucleus of ice or dust and coalesce with supercooled water vapor. As molecules adhere, the vapor freezes and is added to the crystalline structure.

Snow crystal

RAIN, precipitation in liquid form, occurs when tiny droplets are enlarged, first by condensation, then by aggregation with other droplets during their descent. Unless raindrops attain a certain minimum size — about $1/125$ of an inch — they evaporate before reaching the earth.

Raindrop

CONDENSATION, the change from a vapor to a liquid, occurs when the independent molecules in water vapor cool and condense on microscopic dust and salt particles suspended in the air. As more droplets clump together and the air becomes supersaturated, clouds form. On the average, a molecule of water spends nine days in the atmosphere.

Water droplet

GLACIER

MELTWATER

LAKE

GROUNDWATER

GROUNDWATER, held in the openings of permeable bedrock, creeps slowly but steadily to lower levels under the force of gravity. The volume of fresh water stored in the earth is more than two million cubic miles.

States, a 156,000-square-mile swath of subterranean sand and gravel known as the Ogallala aquifer stretches from the edge of South Dakota southwestward into Texas.

Aquifer water follows gravity downhill just as rivers do. Unlike river flow, however, the water in aquifers generally moves through pores in the rock formation, and not through channels. And the water twists and turns through the pores of the aquifer at a tortuously slow pace compared with the flow of even the most sluggish stream.

Hydrologists, the scientists who study the dynamics of water, sometimes resort to the phrase "at a snail's pace" to describe the movement of groundwater. But according to a patient California geologist named John Mann, this estimation is not quite accurate. Mann took a yardstick and stopwatch out to his garden and actually timed a snail's rate of locomo-

Harvesting a stream's bounty, thousands of Nigerians swarm into the Sokoto River with hand nets and gourds, which serve both as flotation devices and as containers for the catch. The local ruler permits fishing on only one day in the dry season, when the river is at its shallowest and fish weighing up to 200 pounds seek refuge in the few remaining deep pools.

tion. Groundwater, he concluded tongue in cheek, moves at an average speed of about 1/70 of a snail's pace.

In fact, hydrologists long have possessed a mathematical formula for calculating precisely how fast underground water travels. It was worked out in 1856 by a Frenchman, Henry Darcy, who was town engineer for Dijon. From measuring the height of water in wells and from other observations, Darcy concluded that one major factor in aquifer flow was the permeability of the rock. Sedimentary rocks such as sandstone and limestone, for example, are highly permeable because they contain innumerable pores through which water can move. Even basalts and other volcanic rocks also can transmit water because of tiny pockets formed by trapped bubbles of volcanic gases. Granite and other dense igneous rocks transmit poorly unless they contain many cracks. Interestingly, the sedimentary rock shale is highly porous but not very permeable because its openings are small and fail to line up with one another. The water has nowhere to go.

Darcy found that other factors affect the flow of groundwater. Rate of flow is directly proportional to the vertical difference in elevation between any two locations on the aquifer, and inversely proportional to the horizontal distance between them. Modern researchers still rely on this formulation, which has come to be known as Darcy's Law. They also trace the speed and route of groundwater by injecting dyes into it or by the application of radioactive-dating techniques. They have learned that aquifer water seldom moves faster than a few inches a day and may travel only a few feet in an entire year.

Groundwater may travel several hundred miles and thus be thousands of years old before making its reappearance on the surface. It may leave its aquifer by several different exits. The most familiar exit is an artificial well dug or drilled to tap the aquifer. Groundwater also discharges naturally into springs wherever the water table intersects with the surface.

Ordinarily, groundwater makes a peaceful exit into wells or springs, seeping gradually out of its aquifer. In some places, however, it jets out of the ground like a geyser. A well with groundwater under pressure is called artesian — from the French province of Artesium, where the ancient Roman conquerors found fountains of water spurting from wells. Artesian springs and wells commonly occur where an aquifer — of sandstone, for example — is sandwiched between layers of shale or some other impermeable rock. This confinement creates the necessary hydraulic pressure to push the water out of the ground at any opening that taps the aquifer.

Artesian springs furnish the only natural flow of water in most deserts. The water, perhaps originating as rainfall hundreds of miles away from the spring, enters a confined aquifer that slopes downward. There, pressure builds up under the weight of the water above and behind. The pressure is relieved when the aquifer intersects the eroded desert floor, or when fractures or faults in the rock allow the water to surge to the surface. This ancient groundwater then spurts free, nurturing an oasis of trees and other vegetation. Springs of either the artesian or ordinary variety often feed rivers. The water may trickle over the ground, giving birth to a stream, or simply supplement the flow of an existing river.

More often, groundwater seeps unseen directly into the channel beneath the river's surface. This direct seepage sustains the flow of many rivers that otherwise would dry up if they had to depend solely upon fresh rainfall. At any given moment, all the world's rivers contain a total of about 300 cubic miles of water — enough on the average to sustain their flow for only about two weeks, and perhaps for only a few hours in arid regions.

The relationship between aquifer and river is not necessarily one-sided. A kind of two-way traffic sometimes takes place, especially in areas where there is little rainfall. The aquifer discharges water into the stream only if the aquifer itself is relatively full. If the water level in the aquifer falls below the level of the river, water tends to move in reverse — out of the river and into the aquifer. A dramatic example in the Southwestern United States is the lower Colorado River, which, flowing southward through the deserts of Arizona, Nevada and Southern California, often supplies water to dried-up aquifers, and they in turn sustain the narrow band of vegetation lining the river.

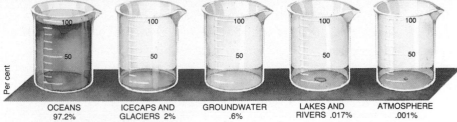

Per cent

| OCEANS 97.2% | ICECAPS AND GLACIERS 2% | GROUNDWATER .6% | LAKES AND RIVERS .017% | ATMOSPHERE .001% |

Rain water, brought to earth during a storm over Alaska's Noatak River, begins its journey back to the ocean, which is the source of nearly all the water in the hydrologic cycle. As shown by the five beakers at right, the combined volume of all the water in lakes and rivers, icecaps and glaciers, atmosphere and ground amounts to only 2.8 per cent of the earth's supply; but even that small percentage totals more than nine million cubic miles of water.

A U.S. Park Service research assistant at Mammoth Cave National Park in Kentucky marks a stream with green fluorescein dye. The dye, carried underground through a sinkhole to distant springs, helps scientists study the speed and the flow pattern of the water.

Groundwater seepage supplies most lakes. Unless the basin consists of impermeable bedrock or is sealed by tight layers of clay or silt sediments, a lake is essentially a surface manifestation of the local water table. Until recently, the aquifers' contributions to lakes were often overlooked by researchers because groundwater seepage into a larger body of water is diffuse and difficult to measure.

But in 1978 this exchange of water was documented in a classic experiment by Canadian hydrologists. First they injected a salt solution a few feet into the ground near Perch Lake in Ontario. Later they measured the salt concentration of water on the lake bed and found that it had increased significantly. They concluded that the salt solution had moved horizontally through the aquifer, curved gently upward and then entered the lake, diffusing throughout an area about six times as large as the place where it had been injected.

The fourth and most important source of water for most rivers and lakes is runoff from precipitation that falls on the land. Runoff occurs when the soil is so saturated that it will not absorb any more water. Rainfall collects on the surface and begins flowing downhill in a broad, shallow sheet usually only a fraction of an inch thick. Soon it funnels into rills, or small channels, which have been dredged by previous runoff. Rills run together to form larger gullies that eventually feed the runoff into a lake or, more commonly, into a river system. There, the runoff joins water supplied by the other stages in the hydrologic cycle. Then the total flow will either evaporate or be carried by a river system to the sea for evaporation (oceans account for 86 per cent of the earth's evaporation) and thus continue the pattern of perpetual circulation.

A river system is composed of all the tributary streams that successively converge to form the main trunk. From the very moment when water enters the system, it is constantly seeking the lowest level, a tendency that leads it back to the sea.

Each component stream in a river system has its own drainage basin, or watershed — the area that funnels its runoff and groundwater downhill into the stream channel. Each watershed is bounded by a ridge, or divide. Every river system has its own divide, and even continents have divides. In the United States, the Continental Divide runs roughly north and south through the Rocky Mountains, separating the rivers that flow toward the Pacific Ocean from those that flow toward the Atlantic or the Gulf of Mexico. River systems follow certain rules in the way their networks of streams are organized. For example, tributaries always join

At the beginning of an eruption, the geyser Strokkur in Iceland heaves up a two-foot-high dome of hot water and starts to eject a thick pillar of steam that can rise 100 feet. Unlike the Strokkur, which erupts every 15 minutes, most geysers erupt at irregular intervals — in whatever time it takes for groundwater in contact with molten rock to build up a greater amount of steam pressure than the underground chambers can contain.

with streams of equal or larger size, much like branches in a tree.

A basic measure for this treelike (or dendritic) organization was formulated during the 1930s by the noted American hydraulic engineer Robert E. Horton. Horton designated each stream by its place in the overall scheme of a river system, with the key to his concept being the number of tributaries feeding a given stream.

Horton classified a stream that has no tributaries as a stream of the first order. When two streams of the first order converge, they form a stream of the second order. But a second-order stream does not pass into the third order, regardless of its number of first-order tributaries, until it unites with another second-order stream. The joining of two third-order streams creates a fourth-order stream, and so on. A river of Mississippi size and complexity is classed as a 10th-order stream; this is the highest order found in North America.

Horton also demonstrated that as a river system advances downstream, the number of tributaries decreases and each tributary becomes longer, deeper and wider—all in a predictable geometric progression. Horton's formulation enables hydrologists to predict the ratio of streams between one order and the next. A typical river system contains about five times as many first-order streams as it does second-order streams.

Other schemes for classifying rivers have been developed using characteristics such as the chemistry or biology of the stream. One classification system, proposed in 1971, involved 13 parameters, each subdivided into

Stream sources of the Waitara River in New Zealand typify the dendritic (treelike) drainage pattern often seen in plains and plateaus. In this most common of drainage patterns, many small streams flow together to form fewer large ones, until all the streams in the watershed converge into one main river.

four to six categories. This made it theoretically possible to define 180 million different types of streams, an impressive feat but one that a prominent researcher called "little more useful than listing them by name."

Horton's method has proved of practical value. In one instance, it helped researchers track down the source of a toxic chemical that had been discovered near the mouth of a river. Statistical analysis of the branching of the different-order tributaries quickly eliminated large sections of the drainage basin as a possible source. This enabled the scientists to narrow their search without having to take water samples from every tributary.

The treelike pattern that typifies river systems is no accident but rather an illustration of nature's efficiency. Luna B. Leopold, former chief hydrologist of the U.S. Geological Survey, points out that the circulatory system in humans and other mammals exhibits similar branching. In trees, rivers and blood vessels, he writes, the pattern tends to keep the total length of the branches at a minimum — and thus minimizes the energy expended by the system.

The main trunk of the river system conducts the most water — usually to the sea but not always. Many rivers empty into lakes; a few disappear into underground caverns or, especially in arid regions, flow to the lowest point in the area and then evaporate.

The biggest of the main trunks bear the familiar names: the Nile, of course, the Amazon, the Zaire (formerly the Congo), the Mississippi, the Yangtze, the Ganges, the Volga, and the enormous but less well-known Rio de la Plata-Paraná of South America. They rank among the score of largest rivers in the world. Together, the top 20 drain about 30 per cent of the world's land area. And every year, they deliver to the sea an estimated 8,000 cubic miles of water — nearly 40 per cent of the combined discharge of all the rivers reaching the ocean.

The indisputable queen of these giants is the Amazon. Though it is second to the Nile in length (3,900 versus 4,160 miles), the Amazon by every other measure ranks as the earth's super-river. Its far-flung system is made up of no fewer than 1,000 streams. At least a score of its principal tributaries exceed 600 miles in length and would be ranked as major rivers in their own right anywhere else. The system drains an area of 2,722,000 square miles — more than one third of the entire continent and nearly twice the watershed of its nearest competitor, the Zaire. The Amazon carries nearly one fifth of all the river water in the world, pumping its discharge into the Atlantic at the prodigious rate of up to five million cubic feet per second — three times that of the Zaire and eight times that of the Mississippi.

Though the Amazon maintains the treelike pattern characteristic of most river systems, everything about the river looms so large and complex as to defy conventional network analysis. Hydrologists cannot even agree whether it is a 12th-order or a 13th-order stream. The system rises in the Peruvian Andes only 100 miles from the Pacific Ocean and attracts tributaries from five other nations to the north and south before the main trunk crosses the whole of Brazil as it flows eastward to the Atlantic. During its course through Brazil, the Amazon receives an average annual precipitation of eight feet, a deluge that periodically sends the river out of its banks and on to the broad flood plain flanking it for distances of up to 30 miles on either side. It is no wonder that early Portuguese voyagers, sailing up this flooded expanse with no land in sight, called the Amazon *Rio Mar* — The River Sea.

The flood plain, which is inundated for several months each year, is a mapmaker's nightmare. It is laced with unusual features labeled with a unique nomenclature. There are *paranás,* or streams that leave and reenter the river; and *igarapés,* narrow channels between two islands or between an island and the mainland, that appear and disappear with the rise and fall of the river, quickly making nautical maps obsolete.

Another feature of the Amazon flood plain is the *cocha,* or "oxbow lake." *Cochas* are the only true lakes in the river's entire drainage basin, and they range up to 60 miles long and 24 miles wide. They are formed when the river carves a new straight channel at one of its great bends, cutting off the length of curved section that doubles back on itself. The *cocha* then stagnates until the annual flood, which replenishes its waters.

A maze of waterways in the Rio Negro section of the Amazon basin turns the landscape into an inland archipelago, creating a navigator's nightmare. These waterways, some of them dead ends, are formed by river currents slicing through vast deposits of sediment brought down from the mountains to the north.

A 12-foot-high tidal bore, called a *pororoca* (or "big roar") in Brazilian Indian, thunders upstream from the mouth of the Amazon with a force that can uproot trees along the banks. This rare phenomenon occurs when the tug of lunar gravity causes a shallow, narrow section of a river to turn back on itself and flow against its own current, away from the sea.

Although the waters of rivers and lakes stem ultimately from the same hydrologic cycle, the basins that contain them derive from radically different beginnings. Rivers are active participants in their own creation, constantly carving out their own channels; indeed, the awesome power of running water, present and past, is largely responsible for shaping many of the earth's continental landscapes. Lakes, by contrast, are essentially passive receptacles, the handiwork of external mechanisms that either produced depressions in the surface of the earth or simply dammed up existing valleys.

How a lake was formed typically dictates its size and three-dimensional shape; these factors, in turn, greatly influence the life of the lake. For example, lakes created by tectonic forces — shifts in the earth's crust — often have U-shaped or V-shaped basins that are deep and steep-sided and relatively poor in plant and animal life. On the other hand, basins created by glacial action tend to be shallow. Because a proportionately higher percentage of their waters comes in contact with nutrient-rich sediments on the bottom of the basins, shallow lakes tend to be more productive biologically.

The genesis of the basin is so important to scientists that they often classify a lake by its origin. One eminent authority, G. Evelyn Hutchinson of Yale University, discerns no fewer than 76 types of lakes, which he groups in 11 major categories on the basis of the particular mechanism that formed them.

A half dozen of Hutchinson's categories include types of lake basins that are relatively rare. Among these are basins created where wind-blown sand dammed up streams in a valley, an American lake that filled such a basin is Moses Lake in the state of Washington. Streams in other valleys have been impounded by landslides of soil and rock; a landslide sealed the basin of the only permanent natural body of water in the Victorian highlands of Australia, Lake Tali Karng. Erosion and deposit of sediments by rivers are responsible for several different types of lakes, including the oxbow lakes left by meandering rivers. Groundwater also carved basins by dissolving great holes in underground limestone beds and causing the overlying rock to collapse. The result is a sinkhole. In the arid Yucatan Peninsula of Mexico, steep-sided sinkholes, known as *cenotes,* have long been important sources of fresh water. A thousand years ago and more, sinkholes were so vital to the Maya Indians that they considered them sacred and built temples nearby.

Some of the most beautiful and strikingly symmetrical lakes stem from volcanic mechanisms. One type, such as Lac d'Issarlès in France and Lake Pulvermaar in West Germany, originated with subterranean explosions that left deep depressions. Another type of lake nestles in a volcano's collapsed crater, or caldera. The most notable example is Oregon's Crater Lake; with a depth of 1,983 feet, it is the deepest body of water in the United States. Its circular basin was formed 7,000 years ago, after a powerful eruption that shattered the surrounding volcano. A later upwelling of lava adorned the lake with a single central island.

Another type of volcanic basin comes into being when lava blocks river valleys. Lava-dammed lakes dot the globe from Guatemala to Turkey and Japan — and keep on appearing. In 1980 lava from Mount St. Helens, in the Cascade Range not far from Crater Lake, created several new lakes; at the same time, however, avalanches of lava and mud obliterated 26 small glacier-carved lakes in the area.

Many of the world's largest, deepest and oldest lakes developed from vertical and horizontal movement of the tectonic plates that make up the earth's crust. Lake Titicaca, athwart the border of Peru and Bolivia, is an example of a lake formed by tectonic uplift. Uplift of surrounding terrain also led to the development of Lake Victoria's basin several million years ago; more recent movements, about 30,000 years ago, tilted the basin and linked its waters with those of the Nile.

Victoria's neighbor, Lake Tanganyika, owes its existence to horizontal sliding of tectonic plates. The plates separated millions of years ago, leaving troughlike grabens more than a mile deep in a lake-studded rift reaching south from the Jordan River for a distance of 4,000 miles. A similar rift in Soviet Asia is responsible for Lake Baikal, which is so deep that it holds one fifth of the world's fresh lake water.

Such prodigious shifts in the earth's crust usually occur over a period of millions of years, but smaller rumblings can give birth to lakes overnight. On February 7, 1812, a series of earthquakes shook a part of the Mississippi River valley, which was then the western frontier of the young American nation. The quakes were so powerful that in some areas the land sank more than 10 feet. Having opened up these basin-like depressions, the trembling earth proceeded to fill them by hurling the river out of its banks. "The Mississippi first seemed to recede from its banks, and its waters gathered up like a mountain," wrote Eliza Bryan, who lived in the nearby river town of New Madrid, Missouri. "Then, rising 15 or 20 feet perpendicularly and expanding, as it were, at the same time, the banks overflowed with a retrograde current rapid as a torrent."

Among the lakes born that day was a 14-mile-long body of water in Tennessee, just across the border from New Madrid. So sudden and violent was its birth that a legend grew up among the local Indians. According to the tale, an Indian chief named Reelfoot — so called because of a foot deformity that forced him to walk with a rolling gait — kidnapped a lovely Indian princess to be his wife. Reelfoot's effrontery provoked the Great Spirit, who stamped his mighty foot, causing the earthquake. A lake formed in his footprint, burying Reelfoot and his stolen bride. To this day the lake is known as Reelfoot.

None of the mechanisms of lake creation — not even earthquakes — can match the slow but enormously powerful creep of glaciers. The process of glacial erosion accounts for 20 of the 76 different types of basin formation in Hutchinson's list. Indeed, it is responsible for more lakes than all the other geological processes combined.

Most of the glacier-made basins are less than 25,000 years old. They date from the most recent ice age, when immense ice sheets advanced over much of the upper latitudes of the Northern Hemisphere, wiping out lakes formed by previous glaciations and creating new ones. In countless numbers, these lakes dapple the landscapes of Scotland and England, Norway, Sweden, Finland, Canada and the Northern United States. The state of Alaska alone boasts of more than three million lakes with surface areas greater than 20 acres.

The mile-thick ice sheets built many basins simply by bulldozing everything in their path. The sheer weight of ice, in combination with the grind-

Two noose-shaped oxbows form along the Huallaga River in Peru, showing just how circuitously this Amazon tributary meandered before carving its new shortcut channel. Oxbows often dry up after being cut off, and their sediment-rich soil fosters loops of lush greenery.

ing action of embedded boulders and other abrasive material, stripped away the soil and scoured the bedrock. The ponderous progress of the ice scooped out the deep basins of the long, narrow fjord lakes along the coasts of Scandinavia — among them Norway's 1,700-foot-deep Hornindalsvatn, the deepest lake in Europe. The glacial bulldozer, aided by tectonic mechanisms, also excavated the largest interconnected system of inland waters in the world, the Great Lakes of North America.

The ice sheets and glaciers turned out to be prolific basin builders in another way as well. As the ice sheets melted and receded, they left behind deposits of rock, soil and sand, known generally as glacial drift. Broad, thick deposits, called moraines, often dammed up rivers. In New York State, moraines plugged both ends of valleys already deepened by glacial scouring and thus formed the 11 Finger Lakes.

Other moraines, spread out like blankets over the scoured bedrock, became receptacles for blocks of ice that broke off from the retreating glaciers. Insulated by the drift, these landlocked icebergs sometimes required hundreds of years to melt. When they finally disappeared, they left their distinctive marks in the soft drift: shallow, kettle-shaped basins now known as kettle lakes.

The dramatic climate changes that gave birth to the ice sheets reached far beyond the ice's advancing tongues. In normally arid regions, precipitation increased so radically that nearly every topographic depression in Asia, western North America and even the African Sahara was filled with water

35

and became, temporarily at least, a full-fledged lake. Later, as temperatures rose and precipitation declined, these so-called pluvial lakes dried up or shrank and turned saline, as did North America's Great Salt Lake. California's Death Valley, now the hottest, driest place in the United States, is actually the graveyard of a pluvial lake that stood there, 180 feet deep, about 20,000 years ago.

Geological forces are not the only lake-builders, of course. For tens of thousands of years, beavers have been felling trees and laboriously constructing log dams that impound the waters of small streams. Human beings began building artificial lakes about 5,000 years ago. And there is also an extraterrestrial lake-building mechanism: impact by meteorites. These few meteorite lakes are rare and stand out sharply because of their precisely circular shapes. Ordinarily, calculating the surface area of a lake is difficult because of its irregular configuration. But Canada's meteorite-caused Lake Chubb presents an easy problem in mathematics: It consists of a near-perfect circle with a diameter of two miles. Another well-known basin excavated by an exploding meteorite, Arizona's Meteor Crater, contained a pluvial lake that dried up about 11,000 years ago, leaving sediments more than 100 feet deep.

Some lakes seem to fit none of the known categories. For decades, geologists have puzzled over the origins of nearly 500,000 small, shallow basins, many of which no longer contain water, that dot the sandy Atlantic coastal plain from Florida as far north as New Jersey. Since glaciers never advanced that far south and there is no evidence of tectonic origin, some scientists suggest that the basins might have been formed by the shock wave accompanying an enormous shower of meteorites. Other hypotheses range from wind action to the motion of schools of fish that, while nesting there when the region lay under shallow seas, somehow scooped out the indentations.

The origin of the myriad coastal-plain basins is but one of the many mysteries still confronting the science of limnology (from the Greek *limnos,* meaning "pool," "lake" or "swamp," and hence, generally, inland waters). As a full-fledged science, limnology is only about a century old. When it evolved during the late 19th Century, geologists already had worked out the mechanisms responsible for most types of lake basins.

In fact, the acknowledged father of limnology, François Forel of Switzerland, was a geologist, physician and naturalist. Forel put his many interests and talents to work in carrying out the first comprehensive study of the physical, chemical and biological characteristics of a lake. In 1892, at the age of 51, he published the first volume in his three-volume study of Lake Geneva. A decade later, he published the first textbook on limnology, which he defined as "the oceanography of lakes."

Later, the science broadened to embrace the study of all inland waters, rivers as well as lakes. A synthesis of many scientific disciplines — hydrology, geology, chemistry, physics and biology — limnology has become increasingly important as civilization encroaches upon inland waters everywhere. It finds practical application in preventing floods, in providing clean water supplies and, above all, in combating pollution and other abuses.

Yet, for all their erudition and sophisticated research techniques, many limnologists are romantics. They are drawn to inland waters by the same

A crater lake on Corvo, the northernmost island in the Azores, covers the floor of a volcano, which collapsed into an empty magma chamber. Since the round basin (or caldera) had no outlet, rain water collected, creating the lake.

ineffable lure that attracted the early explorers of the Nile — what one limnologist has described as "the limnetic drive" in human nature.

A prime example is the Polish-born limnologist Julian Rzóska. In 1946 Rzóska accepted a university post in Khartoum, the Sudanese capital that stands where the Blue Nile and the White Nile join on the way to the sea. Although his limnological experience was limited to lakes in Poland, Rzóska was urged to do a study on the biology of the Nile. Rzóska rented a rowboat and began collecting river specimens with a homemade net. By the time he left Khartoum to teach in London in 1958, his modest project had blossomed into a major research center, complete with its own large motor launch.

Rzóska went on to study other large rivers and to become a widely recognized authority. But, as he wrote later, "the spell of the great river" never left him. Two decades afterward, Rzóska returned to the Nile through his old research notes, writing a fascinating little book called *On the Nature of Rivers*. Like Speke, Burton and the other prominent explorers who had preceded him, this modern limnologist had learned the truth of the ancient Egyptian proverb:

"He who once drinks the water of the Nile will return to drink again."Ω

MASTER SCULPTORS OF THE TERRAIN

For millions of years, rivers have inscribed their life stories on the earth in exquisite detail, gouging out canyons, building up new landforms of mud and stone, and whittling solid rock into pillars and arches. Compared with volcanoes and earthquakes, which can quickly build mountains or crumble whole landscapes, rivers shape the land slowly and peacefully. Yet they are a shaping force more pervasive and powerful than the violent agents of change.

Rivers do their work by three methods: eroding rock and soil, transporting it and depositing it downstream. In general, erosion is extensive where rivers move swiftly and transport substantial quantities of abrasive materials; and deposition takes place where the streams slow down. Naturally, the amount of abrasive debris that a stream can carry depends mainly on the speed of the current and largely determines the erosive power of the river. The sheer force of running water can swiftly carry off soft materials, such as soil and clay, as well as uncompacted sand and gravel.

Erosion works its way not only by these mechanical processes but also by subtle chemical means. Substances in solution in running water leach soluble materials out of rock, weakening the structure and making it more vulnerable to the tearing of the current and the chipping action of the freezing-and-thawing cycle. No less than 3.85 billion tons of dissolved material are transported each year by the world's rivers.

Working by all these methods, a river carries a prodigious volume of material in a short period. For example, the Mississippi transfers more than 440 million tons of silt, clay and sand in an average year. This is enough debris to move its delta six miles seaward every century.

Rainbow Bridge in southern Utah is a span of rock 275 feet long and 290 feet high. It was formed when a river, winding through a deep canyon, cut through a spur of sandstone. Thereafter, the hole under the stone arch was enlarged by the smooth fracturing of curved surfaces and by wind-blown sand and dust.

The Knife River curls through a deep, boldly curved canyon that the stream has cut into the Valley of Ten Thousand Smokes in Alaska. In carving the canyon,

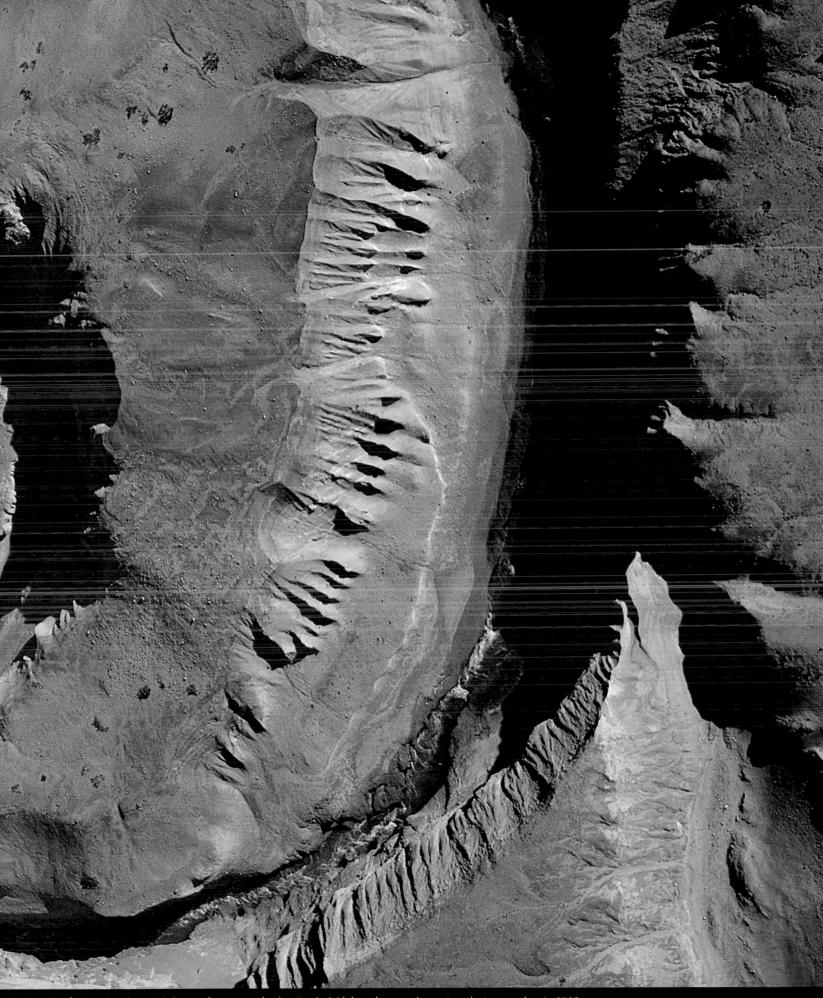

the river sliced through at least nine layers of compressed volcanic ash, laid down by several eruptions during two days in 1912.

A limestone riffle, laid bare during low water, displays the imprint of complex eddies made by the Colorado River in the Grand Canyon. This pattern was carved by the river's abrasive load of sediment, swirling into every crevice and hollow along the watercourse.

An undulating sandstone channel in northern Arizona marks the path of a desert stream that flows only during flash floods. This so-called slot, sculpted by the rough particles suspended in the short-lived but torrential floodwaters, meanders downslope toward the Colorado River. Hundreds of slots drain the 150,000 square miles of the Colorado Plateau.

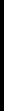

This expanse of jagged spires and columns
near the Bolivian capital of La Paz illustrates the
varied effect of running water on stone of two
different consistencies. The top layer of hard volcanic rock resisted erosion, while an under-
layer of softer sedimentary rock yielded to deep
scouring by water that was racing down
from the highlands of the Andes.

A small stone nests in the pothole it has
helped to excavate in a larger rock. When the
stream rises and flows over the spot, its rotat-
ing motion agitates the smaller, trapped stone
and uses it to abrade and deepen the pothole.

Laden with dissolved calcium carbonate, the blue-green waters of Havasu Creek in Grand Canyon National Park gradually build up deposits that are known as travertine. Residue from the spray of Havasu Falls forms the rocky mantles of travertine that drape the cliff face. In the creek itself, the deposits of travertine take the shape of rounded rims.

An alluvial fan is formed by a seasonal stream in the Peruvian Andes. The stream, rushing downslope through the narrow mountain channel in the background, loses speed as it abruptly reaches the broad river plain in the foreground. There it drops the sediment that it can no longer carry at its diminished velocity. Coarser, heavier particles are unloaded first at the upper part of the alluvial fan. Then fine, light silt is spread out along the lower edge, where the stream joins the broader river.

A New Zealand river, steadily deepening its channel, leaves behind a series of terraces above its banks like a massive staircase. Each step marks the level of a flood plain across which the river flowed earlier in its evolution.

Chapter 2

RIVERS AT WORK

Blondin, the daredevil circus performer from France, outdid himself on June 30, 1859. He strung a 1,000-foot wire 165 feet above the Horseshoe Falls section of Niagara Falls; the tightrope stretched from Goat Island, near the American side of the Niagara River, to the cliff-edged Canadian shore. With spectators on both sides gasping and cheering, Blondin calmly walked across the wire. The crowd's approval and the thorough press coverage were so gratifying to Blondin that he returned for an encore the following year. This time he carried a small stove, and balancing nonchalantly way out there on the high wire, he cooked an omelet.

Thousands came to watch Blondin's death-defying performances. But a far greater attraction has been the falls itself, which draws more than five million visitors a year from all over the world. At 176 feet high and 2,200 feet wide, Niagara Falls is in no way the greatest waterfall; Angel Falls in Venezuela is nearly 20 times as high and Victoria Falls, on the Zambezi River in southern Africa, is two and one half times as wide. But Niagara Falls has a steady year-round flow and an accessible location, and with its magnificent natural amphitheater for viewing, it is the most convenient place to watch and listen to a mighty river at work.

By geologists' reckoning, the Niagara River has been working for about 12,000 years. It emerged after the retreat of the last great ice sheet and ever since has carried billions of gallons of water a year from Lake Erie to Lake Ontario. As it thunders downslope on its 35-mile course, the Niagara batters everything in its path, particularly the cliff that creates the falls.

The cliff is part of the Niagara Escarpment, a ridge that once underlaid the channel of the river for most of its length. The top of the ridge consists of dolomite, a durable, erosion-resistant type of limestone. But the river found a way to undermine the hard cap rock, and this subversive process continues today.

Many observers mistakenly assume that the cliff is undercut by the erosive power of turbulent water at the base of the falls. The turbulence there has, in fact, excavated a plunge pool 100 feet deep. But the undercutting process is more subtle. Upstream from the falls, water seeps into cracks in the dolomite, weakening the layers of softer shales below it. The undercut dolomite gives way, crumbling into small pieces or sometimes breaking off in enormous slabs up to 150 feet long that crash thunderously into the pool below.

As a result, the falls have retreated more than seven miles in 12,000 years, leaving a narrow gorge of that length. Until the 1950s the annual

Angel Falls on the Río Caroní in Venezuela spills 3,212 feet down the sandstone face of a towering plateau. The waterfall, named for American soldier of fortune Jimmy Angel, who discovered it in 1935, is the world's highest.

rate of retreat ranged from three to six feet. Since then the rate has been slowed by the diversion of 75 per cent of the river water upstream from the falls. A year-round average of about 150,000 cubic feet of water per second is diverted into four large tunnels — two on each side of the American-Canadian border — that carry the water downhill to turn hydroelectric turbines. These turbines convert the energy of the river into 2,400 megawatts, enough electricity to light almost two million homes.

This restriction on the river's work load has reduced the falls' rate of retreat to a foot or two per year. The river now has about 20 miles of dolomite ridge to undermine before the falls retreat to Lake Erie, an eventuality that will require more than 50,000 years at the present rate of erosion. Even then, when the prodigious cadence of the falls is at last silenced, the river will continue to scour its channel and cart away the debris.

All rivers, even the laziest streams, are constantly shaping the surface of the earth. They excavate their valleys, transport soil and rocky debris, deposit new landforms and incessantly rework their own channels. In all this work, rivers expend enormous amounts of energy — by one estimate, 100 times the total produced by man-made energy-generating projects.

Rivers derive their energy from the simple fact of their elevation. Like the waters at Niagara, if less spectacularly, other rivers are always falling, flowing downhill toward their ultimate base level, the sea. Naturally, the fastest river velocities have been recorded at waterfalls: A flow of 100 feet per second — 68 miles per hour — has been measured on the Niagara. High current speeds have been recorded just below waterfalls. On South America's Paraná River, currents up to 45 feet per second — 30 miles per hour — occur just below the 100-foot-high Guaíra Falls. On the average, however, streams flow at the leisurely rate of three to six feet per second, or two to four miles per hour.

The obvious role of gravity in determining the velocity of running water has led to a widespread misconception — that torrential mountain streams flow swiftly, while broad rivers roll along slowly. In fact, water velocity often increases downstream despite the loss of steep slope. For example, the River Tweed, Scotland's second-largest river, has precipitous mountain streams for its headwaters, while its broad lower stretches flow down a much gentler gradient. Though the headwaters apparently move faster, a 10-year study by David C. Ledger of the University of Edinburgh showed otherwise. In widely contrasting sections of the river system he set up current meters, whose propellers are turned by the water's flow and thus measure stream speed. These meters showed that the velocity of the Tweed generally increased downstream, just where it appeared to be slower.

The effects of friction account for this anomaly. Friction of the river rubbing against its bed and banks usually lessens downstream because erosion has smoothed the stream bed there, facilitating the flow. More important, the river widens and deepens downstream as tributaries join it and the mass of water increases; consequently, a greater proportion of the volume flows friction free. The broad lower Amazon, for example, reaches speeds of up to eight feet per second — faster than many mountain torrents whose channels slope more precipitously.

Rivers lose up to 97 per cent of their energy to various types of friction — with the air, with the stream bed and within the turbulent water itself.

When a Mighty Waterfall Ran Dry

The American Falls lies dry after a cofferdam was built to divert the Niagara River. Exposed here are the falls's escarpment, capped by erosion-resistant dolomite, and the tons of debris that have collapsed at its base.

In 1969 the United States and Canada committed more than two million dollars to an extraordinary project: stopping the flow of the American section of Niagara Falls. The project was launched to permit a close study of the escarpment above the American Falls and to remove the immense jumble of talus, or broken rock, accumulated at its base.

Engineers built a cofferdam and diverted the river's flow from the American Falls to the much larger Horseshoe Falls on the Canadian side. They cleared sediment from a section of the channel, exposing the fractures, or joints, in the stream-bed rock. Geologists mapped the fractures in the chan-

The American Falls (*foreground*) flows again after the Niagara River was temporarily diverted. Higher than the Horseshoe Falls on the Canadian side, the American Falls accounts for less than one tenth of the river's flow.

nel and the horizontal face of the falls and took sample borings to analyze the characteristics of the rock.

The plan to remove the talus was abandoned as alien to the natural evolution and beauty of the falls. The cofferdam was removed, and the thundering Niagara returned to its normal channel.

As a result of the study, steps were taken to retard further erosion, particularly in tourist areas. Above the falls, steel bolts up to 40 feet long were driven into the rock to strengthen weak joints along the river bank. A popular observation point, in danger of collapse, was made safe by inserting bolts and blasting away some of the overhanging rock.

Nevertheless, the rivers of the world retain enough usable energy to remove an annual average of nearly two tons of soil and rock from every square mile of terrain. This amounts to lowering the entire land surface of the earth by three inches every 1,000 years.

Running water constantly remodels the land by a combination of three different mechanisms. One mechanism is chemical erosion. Reacting chemically with the rocks it touches, river water dissolves and carries off mineral compounds known as salts. The presence of these salts is seldom evident to the naked eye. They are carried in the form of ions — tiny electrically charged parts of a molecule. Rock gypsum, for example, contains the compound calcium sulfate. When dissolved in water, it yields calcium ions and sulfate ions. Calcium compounds, along with certain other salts, give water its taste. They also make for hard water, which leaves a bothersome scale on the inside of the home hot-water tank and combines with laundry soap to form insoluble deposits in the weave of cloth.

Dissolved salts constitute a substantial portion of the load that rivers transport. As the Niagara River sweeps over Niagara Falls, it carries an average of 60 tons of dissolved minerals a minute.

The rate of chemical erosion depends upon the resistance of the rock and the solvent power of the water. Limestone is the most soluble of the major rocks; granite and lava generally resist solution. Water's solvent action increases with the absorption of carbon dioxide from the air. The ability of water to dissolve is also enhanced by dissolved organic acids acquired from decaying vegetation. Groundwater is a potent solvent simply because it moves so slowly and thus remains in contact with an area of rock much longer than impatient rivers. In fact, streams with a high content of dissolved minerals often receive more of their flow from groundwater than from surface runoff.

Another mechanism of erosion is hydraulic action, or the sheer force of running water. A swiftly flowing stream can widen cracks and pry out large chunks of fractured rock. In 1923 a stream at flood stage in the Wasatch Mountains of the Northwestern United States wrenched loose boulders weighing up to 90 tons and carried them more than a mile downstream.

The most powerful type of erosion is abrasion. Sand and pebbles picked up by the stream prove to be highly efficient instruments. They scour the channel's bed and banks. They cut through joints, or fractures, in hard rock. When trapped in depressions and powered by turbulent eddies, they rotate like a drill bit, carving out deep potholes. And boulders acquired by fast currents slam against solid rock like sledgehammers, breaking the rock into smaller pieces that the river can work on with its other tools.

A typical V-shaped valley, the Maruia River valley on South Island, New Zealand, shows the action of a stream steadily deepening its channel by erosion. The Maruia's flow is augmented by 200 inches of rainfall per year, which also steepens the slopes of the valley.

Erosion by these three methods enables a river to widen and deepen its channel and, in time, to create its own valley. Creation of the typical V-shaped valley, however, requires collaboration. Rainfall striking the slope loosens particles of soil and rocky debris. At first, the rain runs off in a thin sheet flow, which moves sluggishly and can carry only the finest particles. But the impact of rain on this sheet flow stirs up sufficient turbulence to move pebbles up to a half inch in diameter.

The erosive force builds as runoff collects in rills and gulleys and then funnels into the river. Meanwhile, rock that has been weakened by frost and other weathering action moves down the slope under the influence of gravity. It reaches the river, is worked over and finally swept away.

A different kind of valley results in regions where, through circumstance of climate or geology, the river itself becomes the predominant force in sculpting the landscape. In these cases, a steep-walled chasm, such as North America's Grand Canyon, takes shape.

The mighty Colorado River, dropping 2,200 feet in its 217-mile course through the canyon, has carved straight down for more than a mile over a period of several million years. But the region's paucity of rainfall and the strength of some strata of rock have prevented formation of gentle slopes. Instead, the canyon presents a stairstep profile of alternating steep slopes and rock terraces.

This profile evolved because the successive rock strata vary greatly in their resistance to erosion. The slopes generally consist of soft shales, while the terraces are limestone and cemented sandstone durable enough to resist erosion by the relatively small amounts of rainfall that wash down the canyon walls.

Erosion is only the beginning of a river's work. Next comes the transportation of the eroded soil and rock downstream. The river expends little energy carrying material in solution; once minerals are dissolved, they remain that way regardless of the velocity of the water. A change in the chemistry of the water rather than in its speed precipitates the salts and causes them to be deposited. Dissolved matter constitutes a surprisingly large proportion of the load that rivers transport to the sea — by some estimates, 50 per cent or more. According to one study, the 16 largest river systems dump 56 tons of minerals into the oceans every second.

Dissolved nutrients, such as iron, calcium and phosphorus, have wide-ranging effects. The nutrients picked up by the Amazon, for example, enrich areas far beyond its own vast flood plain. They are discharged into the Atlantic, are swept northward and eventually fertilize the floating plant life in the Grand Banks off Newfoundland, one of the earth's great fisheries.

Nevertheless, rivers generally carry far more material in suspension than in solution. The Mississippi River, for example, carries about 70 per cent of its eroded material in suspension; this amounts to an annual load of more than 440 million tons. Oddly, mineral salts dominate the Mississippi's upstream load, and the river runs relatively clear. But as the Mississippi winds south toward the Gulf of Mexico, the waters become increasingly turbid with suspended sediments — silt, clay, sand and even rock.

Several rivers are named after the characteristic coloring of the sediments they carry. The Colorado, meaning "red" in Spanish, acquires that color from the reddish sandstone it scours in the Grand Canyon and elsewhere; it carries nearly as hefty a load as the Mississippi while draining a region less than one fifth the size of the Mississippi's watershed.

The biggest color-named carrier of suspended material is China's Huang He, or Yellow River, which transports no less than 10 per cent of the world's riverborne sediments. The river's load — almost all of it the yellowish wind-deposited silt called loess — amounts to 1.6 billion tons annually. On the average, loess represents 46 per cent of the weight of the river, sometimes appearing to reduce the flow to that of molasses. The river has been discolored by loess for so many millennia that the Chinese have coined an idiom equivalent to the English "when hell freezes over": "when the river runs clear."

Highly unusual circumstances shape the Yellow River's enormous burden. Ninety per cent of it comes from a region where the mantle of loess sometimes reaches a depth of more than 500 feet. Insufficient rainfall prevents the growth of enough vegetation to bind this loose silt and retard erosion. And most of the rain falls in a few storms so intense that the copious runoff carves deep gulleys in the loess. These gulleys serve as channels for short-lived streams that wash an astonishing volume of silt into the tributaries and main trunk of the river.

When the load becomes too large for the Yellow River to handle, the excess settles on the bottom. Eventually, the accumulation of silt raises the riverbed to a level where the waters spill out of the channel, setting off one of the catastrophic floods that have earned the river its melancholy renown as "China's sorrow."

A dry stretch of the Lethe River in Alaska *(above)* is strewn with rock and sand that were carried there when the river was swollen by springtime meltwater. Heavier materials, too large to be swept along in suspension and known as the river's bed load *(right),* are a major contributor to erosion. The particles scrape at the riverbed as they are propelled downstream by the current, rolling or sliding or hopping along in a motion called saltation. As the river slows, particles are deposited in order of size, beginning with the largest.

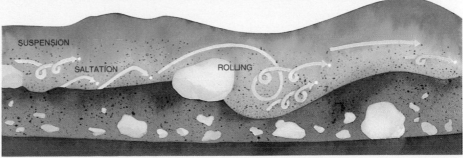

SUSPENSION

SALTATION

ROLLING

Dusted with snow, Utah's Gooseneck Canyon is the product of ages of erosion by the San Juan River. The river, meandering on a plain, cut downward as

the land was thrust upward by tectonic forces. Now flowing 1,500 feet below the canyon's rim, the river travels 25 miles to cover a five-mile distance.

The ability of a river to transport sediment depends in large part on the characteristics of the eroded material. In general, large particles are more difficult to move than small ones. Fine particles of clay are often more resistant to erosion than large grains of sand because of the strong cohesive force that glues the clay together. But once clay particles are dislodged and picked up by a river, they are carried along with much less effort.

The volume and velocity of the river itself are also key factors. Increases in a river's volume during a flood enlarge its carrying capacity. And a speed-up in velocity enables the river to move larger particles. Doubling a stream's speed can produce a fourfold increase in the size of the particles it can carry. This heightened carrying power is a result of greater turbulence in the river, which keeps masses of water swirling erratically even while generally moving downstream.

Intertwined streams wander across the delta formed by the Dart River as it flows into Wakatipu Lake in New Zealand's Humboldt Mountains. These so-called braided streams develop when the sediment load in a river exceeds its ability to move the sediment. The deposits that result block the flow and split the river into a network of smaller branches.

Rivers bear their highest concentrations of suspended load near the bottom. On the stream bed itself, sediment is also being transported — though much more slowly and by a different mechanism. The bed load consists of particles too large to be carried in suspension: large grains of sand, pebbles and perhaps even boulders. As this abrasive load is pushed along by the force of the current, it adds to the stream's power to scour and erode the bedrock bottom.

The bed load travels haltingly. Particles slide, roll or sometimes even skip along in a process known as saltation. A saltating particle is caught by the lift of an upward eddy, briefly joining the fast lane of the suspended load before plunging again to the bottom, where it is relegated once more to the slow-moving bed load.

Though the bed load is difficult to see and measure, the rumble of boulders rolling and bouncing along the bottom can often be heard in swift and shallow mountain streams. Researchers estimate that transport along the bottom ranges from 7 to 10 per cent of the typical river's total load of sediments, but can be as high as 50 per cent.

In the final stage of its never-ending cycle of work, a river deposits the debris it has eroded and carried downstream. Deposition is usually an effortless process; the river merely relinquishes to gravity the load it has borne, gradually forming new terrain features. Once deposited, the material is called alluvium. It is estimated that rivers drop as much as 75 per cent of their alluvium before they reach the sea.

One type of stream-made landform, the alluvial fan, is usually created well upstream in a river system's network of tributaries. When a mountain stream tumbles down onto a plain and enters a slower-moving river, the reduced rate of flow often causes a loss in load. Boulders and fist-sized cobbles settle out first, then sand and finer silts. Over time, the build-up of sediments clogs the channel, forcing the stream to shift its course from side to side. The result is a fan-shaped area of deposit spreading out from the foot of the mountain. Given enough time, fans from a number of neighboring streams may merge into a broad expanse of alluvium. In arid regions of the Western United States, alluvial fans more than 10 miles wide — the legacies of streams that dried up thousands of years ago — adorn the bases of mountain ranges.

Farther downstream in a river system, the features of the flood plain predominate. The flood plain is the wide, flat belt inundated by a stream when it overflows its banks, a phenomenon that occurs two out of every three years in the average river. The flood plain's surface consists in part of alluvium deposited by overflowing waters. The rest of the alluvium has been added by normal flow in old channels that have been abandoned as the river migrates back and forth across its valley, changing course with time.

One of the greatest flood plains is the work of the Mississippi; it was mostly built up before the construction of dams and other flood-control projects brought a measure of restraint to the big river's periodic rampages. Measuring 125 miles across at its widest point, the flood plain embraces about 30,000 square miles of silt-rich farmland extending from the confluence of the Mississippi and Ohio Rivers at Cairo, Illinois, all the way south to New Orleans.

In many stretches of its course through the flood plain, the Mississippi flows between ridges of sediment deposited by its floodwaters. These natural levees, ranging up to 16 feet in height, are formed by a selective grading process. As a broad sheet of water overflows its channel, it loses velocity. The larger sediments settle out first and gradually build up the banks during successive floods. Further decreases in the velocity and volume of the dispersing floodwaters cause finer particles of silt to settle in deposits that thin out as the distance from the river increases.

These levees can help prevent further floods, especially when reinforced with stone and concrete. New Orleans, near the mouth of the river, has reinforced levees 25 feet high. Between these levees, accumulated deposits in the stream bed have actually raised the river channel higher than portions of the city. Visitors to the French Quarter are often surprised — on hearing the horn of a riverboat — to look up at the craft passing along the river.

Alluvium serves as the building material for another kind of flood-plain feature, the river terrace. Steplike terraces stem from a complex sequence of events in which the elevation of a flood plain changes. For example, uplift of the earth's crust may raise the level of the flood plain. The river then erodes a portion of the alluvium previously deposited there and later completely abandons the old flood plain, leaving terraces on either side of its former channel. In the American West, series of terraces often descend the sides of abandoned valleys like majestic stairs.

The most distinctive alluvial landform, the delta, occurs all the way downstream at the river's mouth. When a stream empties into a standing body of water — either a lake or an ocean — the sudden loss of velocity and energy dumps all the remaining load of sediment. The formation of a delta there depends upon the outcome of a contest between the river and the ocean. A delta will be created if the river deposits enough sediment to withstand dispersion by the sea's powerful currents and tides.

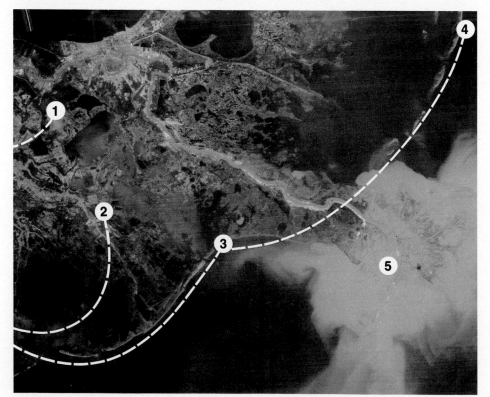

A 1973 satellite photograph of the mouth of the Mississippi River presents an example of a bird's-foot delta, with five lobes projecting into the Gulf of Mexico (*bottom*). Dashed lines mark the older, eroded lobes; superimposed numbers indicate the order in which the lobes were formed during the past 5,000 years. Only the fifth lobe, built up over the past 500 years, is still active, depositing its sediment over the edge of the continental shelf.

Deltas assume several recognizable shapes. The familiar triangular pattern is responsible for the name, which derives from the observation 2,500 years ago by Herodotus that the shape of the land at the mouth of the Nile resembled the Greek letter delta. Many other rivers, such as Africa's Niger, deposit a fan-shaped delta. The Mississippi sends out long talons of alluvium that form the so-called bird's-foot delta.

In the long process of laying down a delta, a river undergoes an unusual transformation. Nearing the sea, the river branches out into a network of streams that resembles — but in reverse — the treelike pattern of tributaries that combine to form the river many miles upstream. These twigs at the river's end, which are called distributaries, play a vital role in allocating material to the deposits in the delta.

The delta-building process typically begins as the river deposits a large bar of sand at the mouth of its channel. The bar gradually mounts in size until it separates the river's flow into two smaller channels. Beginning underwater, the banks of these new channels are built up with alluvium deposited by slow-moving currents that flare out seaward at the periphery of the river's main flow.

The two new distributaries flowing through these lesser channels repeat the process. Each one deposits a sandbar and then divides into two smaller channels, which subdivide in turn. Continuing repetition results in a system of constantly branching streams, all depositing sediments and extending seaward.

A further refinement in delta building has been discovered by researchers studying the Mississippi delta. When the river nears flood stage there, the surging volume in the distributaries breaks through the levees that ordinarily confine them. Deposits from these diverted waters then form what scientists call a splay: a new subdelta with its own little distributaries and — eventually — its own subsplays.

In this manner the Mississippi has constructed five major subdeltas in the past 5,000 years. One of them has eroded and is now all but inundated. But the others protrude talon-like into the Gulf, adding a total of 15,000 square miles of land to what is now the state of Louisiana. This impressive expansion is the gift of the Mississippi, which daily augments its delta with an estimated one million tons of clay, silt and sand.

The landforms shaped by rivers are legacies of thousands, even millions, of years of work. A river's life span often extends over immense periods of time; northern parts of the Colorado system, for example, date back at least 25 million years. Throughout such periods, streams are constantly evolving. External events often intervene. Tectonic processes raise or lower regions of the earth's crust and tilt drainage patterns first one way, then another. Drastic changes in climate dry up entire river systems, rejuvenate others or send massive ice sheets down from the north to bulldoze a stream's channel or block and reverse its drainage with great deposits of debris.

In the meantime, the stream is shaping and changing its own course. Channel changes occur when one stream competes for the territory of another. A swift tributary carving through soft rock can breach the divide that separates it from the drainage basin of a neighboring stream. The headwaters of the neighboring stream will thus be captured and diverted into the channel of the invader.

Geologists of the Victorian age took a moralistic view of such matters and named this process stream piracy. Through stream piracy, an entire river system can be captured by another, drastically altering regional drainage patterns. More commonly, such aggression occurs on a smaller scale and creates many narrow gorges and little valleys where water no longer flows.

Rivers are constantly reshaping the topography of their channel bottoms. Upstream, where the river expends most of its energy carving ever deeper into bedrock, boulders and other large particles may clutter the bed. Downstream, the bed tends to be smooth. By then, the large chunks of sediment pried loose by the turbulent headwaters have been battered and fragmented by their long journey. They are reduced to grains of sand that, along with small particles of silt, settle to the bottom in a kind of temporary storage until they are swept up again to resume the trip seaward.

Stream beds are sometimes crossed with ridge-shaped accumulations of silt or sand known as bars. The force of the current may shape bars into serried ranks not unlike a series of wind-whipped sand dunes on a desert. On major waterways such as the Mississippi and the Amazon, the bars shift rapidly and unpredictably, posing constant hazards for ship pilots. Researchers investigating the lower Amazon have found gigantic bars in the channel that measure 25 feet in height and more than 200 yards in length.

Another type of undulating stream-bed topography occurs most characteristically on rock-strewn bottoms. This pattern consists of riffles — areas of shallow, turbulent water paved with stones or gravel — alternating with deeper pools of slower-moving flow that have bottoms of finer sediments.

During the 1950s, Scottish biologist Thomas A. Stuart recognized the importance of riffles as spawning habitats for trout and salmon. The bubbling flow provides the rich supply of oxygen needed by the eggs of these fish. In the course of his investigations, Stuart was particularly intrigued by the regular spacing of riffles and pools: One each typically occurs in a length of stream equivalent to five to seven widths of its channel.

This observation suggested an unusual experiment. Stuart had piles of gravel placed at these regular intervals in the bed of an artificial stream that was being excavated by a dragline. The new stream began picking up the gravel and eventually distributed it in the characteristic arrangement of riffles and pools.

To learn more about riffle-pool dynamics, two American hydrologists, Luna B. Leopold and M. Gordon Wolman, studied Seneca Creek in Maryland during the 1960s. When the creek was running low, they painted all of the exposed pieces of gravel in a riffle. They returned after a period of high flow and found, as they expected, that all of the marked pieces had moved downstream, some of them as far as the next riffle, while other gravel from the nearest riffle upstream had taken the place of the painted pieces. Though the material in a riffle changed, Leopold and Wolman noted, the location of riffles remained fixed.

Indeed, riffle locations have proved remarkably stable over long periods of time. Studies of Australia's Hawkesbury River, for example, established that its riffle-pool pattern has not changed in a century.

In addition to their effects on the stream bottom, erosion and deposition of sediments help shape the longitudinal pattern of the river channel. Though rivers seem to take many forms, hydrologists distinguish three main types of channel patterns: braided, straight-stream and meandering.

Braided channels develop where the sediment load is too large for the depth of the channel and for the volume of water flowing past a particular point in a given amount of time. The Platte River in Nebraska is a prime example of a stream with many braided channels. There, parallel series of long narrow sandbars deposited by the river separate the main channel into a complex network of smaller channels. In places, the flow breaks through the bars, crisscrossing between channels and giving the characteristic braided appearance when seen from above.

The second type, the straight-stream channel, is surprisingly rare. A straight stretch of channel seldom exceeds a length equal to 10 times its width, even when researchers stretch the definition to allow for minor bends. A section of channel is considered straight if the distance traveled by the stream is less than 1.2 times the direct-line distance. Straight-stream channels commonly occur only in special circumstances. For example, a stream may be prevented from wandering by banks of erosion-resistant rock or by a slope so steep that the stream can only continue its headlong plunge.

Almost all streams have stretches featuring the third type of channel pattern. Instead of taking the straightest line to the sea, they meander—loop in gentle curves—like the river in Turkey, the Menderes, from which the term derives.

The question of how and why rivers meander has long intrigued research-

The Jardine River, meandering through the wilderness of Australia's Cape York Peninsula, erodes soil from its outer bank wherever it swerves swiftly around a bend. The river then deposits part of this sediment load as arc-shaped bars where the current slows.

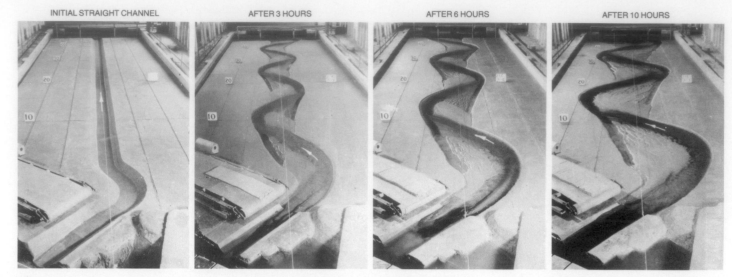

ers. A number of local factors can cause a river to change direction. It may be turned aside by an erosion-resistant rock formation or by a chance obstacle, such as a large boulder or a fallen tree. But such random happenings can hardly account for the striking symmetry of meander bends or for the remarkable similarity of bends in streams of different sizes in diverse physical settings.

The mystery has challenged eminent scientists of many disciplines for decades. One widely held theory proposed that meandering was caused by the Coriolis force, which is exerted by the spinning of the earth upon its axis. But modern research has shown that this force is not sufficient to bend all those rivers.

During the early 1940s an American researcher brought the question into the laboratory. Working at the U.S. Waterways Experiment Station in Vicksburg, Mississippi, Captain Joseph F. Friedkin of the Army Corps of Engineers attempted to simulate conditions in which meandering might develop. He constructed a series of small-scale rivers ranging in width from one to five feet and in length from 50 to 150 feet. These model rivers flowed on floors built of sand and silts, and they were arranged so that Friedkin could vary their slope and the volume of water passing through.

The channels of Friedkin's rivers were straight in the beginning. But soon after he introduced water, they began to change course. A noticeable tendency to meander developed in just three hours. After six hours, the river channels swept back and forth in broad curves. Friedkin concluded that a complicated process involving erosion of stream banks and deposition of sediments was responsible for meandering.

Thanks to the work of Friedkin and many others, the mechanics of floodplain meanders are now reasonably clear. Meanders most commonly occur wherever the river traverses a gentle slope that is covered with fine-grained, easily eroded alluvium. As the stream enters a curve, centrifugal force hurls the faster-moving water near the surface against the concave, or outside, bank of the bend, eroding it.

But the fate of the sediment eroded from the outside bank is determined by the peculiar hydrodynamics of meandering. While the surface water hugs the outside bank, the slower water near the bed compensates for this, tending to move toward the inside bank of the curve. This pattern of circulation across the channel, combined with the general flow downstream,

An artificial river, rigged up at the U.S. Waterways Experiment Station in Vicksburg, Mississippi, presents classic proof of the tendency of flowing water to seek a meandering course. To simulate riverbank erosion, a conveyor belt feeds granular material into the stream, deflecting the current against the far bank. There, the water scours away more material and is deflected back across the channel. In just a few hours of alternately eroding and depositing material along each bank, the straight stream develops a series of sinuous curves.

creates a kind of helical, or corkscrew, motion. As it proceeds downstream, this motion reverses its direction of rotation with each successive meander.

As a result, most of the silt picked up from the outer bank is deposited on the inner bank of the next curve. The arc-shaped deposit of silt that accumulates on the inner bank is called a point bar. As the point bar grows larger, the arc of the curve increases.

This process by which the outer banks are constantly being eroded while the inner banks build up has profound consequences for the location of the river channel. Though the width and cross-sectional shape of its channel generally remain constant, the river slowly executes a kind of side step across the flood plain. As the channel migrates laterally, it leaves behind the alluvium that formerly made up the point bar on the inside bank of each meander. These deposits, together with alluvium left by the river when it periodically overflows its banks, form the surface of the flood plain.

Though it usually takes centuries for a meandering channel to undergo a substantial shift in location, the short lateral movement of a single meander sometimes poses an unexpected threat to human settlements on the flood plain. Such was the plight of the 1,360 residents of the southwestern Indiana city of New Harmony. Since the town's founding in 1813 as a short-lived utopian community of German immigrants, the Wabash River has meandered past its western outskirts, looping lazily toward the northeast.

In 1978, however, Robert Shaver of the Indiana Geological Survey charted a history of the river's successive locations on the flood plain and made an alarming discovery. A meander north of New Harmony, which had long been sidestepping toward the town at a rate of about 18 yards a year, had nearly doubled its pace in recent years. By 1984 the migrating meander had again doubled its rate of erosion and was less than a half mile north of town. At this new pace, the meander will begin undercutting the alluvium on which New Harmony stands by 1994.

To save the town, government engineers must somehow stop the meander's southward migration. One way of accomplishing this is to stabilize the eroding outer bank of the meander with a wall of cement blocks or boulders, at an estimated cost of $500,000. Another, even more expensive option is to reroute the river and thus cut off the troublesome curve altogether. The meander would then be stranded as a harmless oxbow lake.

While river researchers have developed some understanding of the mechanics of meanders, unsettling theoretical questions persist. For example, does erosion actually cause meanders in the first place? Or is the carving of those gentle curves the result of some underlying principle at work in the river?

No researchers have wrestled with these questions more assiduously than Luna Leopold—the hydrologist who showed how gravel migrates from riffle to riffle—and his colleagues at the U.S. Geological Survey. Their work, beginning in the 1950s, tended to focus on the dynamics of stream flow rather than on erosion, which had been the preoccupation of Joseph F. Friedkin in his studies of laboratory rivers.

Friedkin's earlier findings provided a starting point for the new research. He had noted that even in straight channels, stream flow showed a tendency to meander. In some of his experiments, the thalweg—the path followed by the deepest parts of the channel—wandered back and forth between the banks.

Leopold and M. Gordon Wolman, studying streams in the laboratory and in the field, discovered intriguing similarities in the sinuosity of the wandering thalweg. In both straight and meandering channels, its path crisscrossed the channel at fairly regular intervals—at a distance of about five to seven channel widths.

At Dinwoody Glacier in Wyoming's Wind River Range, Leopold and Wolman made an even more interesting discovery. Friedkin had insisted that flowing water must be confined between banks in order to establish a pattern of meandering. On the contrary, they found that as meltwater flowed over the glacier, unconstrained by banks and unaccompanied by sediment, it chiseled into the ice the familiar gentle and geometrically regular curves of a meandering river.

Subsequent observations have established other situations in which flowing water shows the same sinuosity. Currents in the Atlantic Ocean's Gulf Stream meander. Even a small stream of water from a hose meanders when directed over the surface of an inclined piece of glass or porcelain tile.

What is more, the ubiquitous meander pattern shows up in the riffles and pools investigated by Leopold and Wolman. The regularly spaced bars of gravel that give rise to riffles typically do not extend all the way across the width of the stream but jut out alternately from opposite banks. When low water exposes the bars, the flow bends around the end of each one, wandering meander-like from one side of the channel to the other. Leopold and Wolman concluded that erosion is a kind of side effect of meandering, not the first cause. Meanders—and indeed all patterns in the river channel, they suggested—result from variations in a stream's flow and in its slope.

Leopold and other associates went on to delve deeper into the nature of this special curve that characterizes the meander. Computer studies and close observations in the field led them to an interesting analogy. Meander curves are identical to the shapes assumed by a thin strip of spring steel when held in the hands and bent. These configurations allow the steel's expenditure of energy in bending to be uniformly distributed along the length of the curve, minimizing the total work done.

Similarly, Leopold concluded, meandering is actually a kind of energy-saving mechanism. The river is constantly adjusting to variations in its depth, velocity and slope, always working to minimize excesses in the expenditure of energy. The meander actually distributes the stream's work load more uniformly over bed irregularities than does a straight channel.

"In brief," wrote Leopold in 1966, "we have found that meanders are not mere accidents of nature but the form in which a river does the least work in turning, and hence are the most probable form a river can take."

For more than 4,500 years, the same water power that reshapes the landscape has been harnessed by human beings to make their lives easier. The harnessing began in the Middle East with the fashioning of a crude water wheel whose protruding paddles turned a shaft with a millstone mounted on the end. Aided by the river's energy, these pioneers in hydropower were able to grind grain.

Today, enormous dams tame most of the mightiest rivers, producing an estimated one fourth of the world's electricity. In effect, the modern dam creates an artificial waterfall—one that may stand three or four times as high as Niagara Falls, where the first large hydroelectric plant was built in

A citrus grove blooms in the Sonoran Desert east of Yuma, Arizona. This artificial oasis is nourished by water carried to the arid site by a concrete-lined irrigation canal.

Southern California is a virtual desert, where the shortage of water has long been a many-sided problem. Water projects have become a way of life for the region; the cities and farms of Southern California receive water via more than 1,200 dams and a network of diversion channels stretching hundreds of miles from mountains to the north and from the Colorado River to the east.

The southern part of the Colorado River, bordering California and its parched neighbor Arizona, has been a major source of water — and of contention. California has been drinking deeply from the river since the early 1900s, when developers built a canal from the Colorado to support farming in the dry but fertile Imperial Valley. How much of the river California may divert is limited by a signed pact with six other states, by a U.S.-Mexico water-rights treaty and by Supreme Court decisions guaranteeing adequate water to Indian reservations. On occasion the state has tried to take more than its legal share of the Colorado, but in 1964 Arizona won a landmark court case that forced California to look elsewhere for more water.

Watering the desert has also posed technical problems. Irrigation canals have been silted up, and farmlands have been poisoned by mineral salts in the diverted water. These problems, like the water shortage itself, can be solved only at great cost in money and ingenuity. For the foreseeable future, it seems certain that the life-and-death issues of water policy will continue to dominate the politics and economy of the region.

Water from the Sierra Nevada in east central California courses down a 12-foot-wide siphon on its way to a thirsty Los Angeles in the arid southwestern part of the state.

Tall sunflowers, their heavy heads drooping beside an irrigation ditch in Sacramento, are one of the innumerable California crops that consume 85 per cent of the water delivered through California's elaborate diversion system; the other 15 per cent is routed to the cities for household and industrial use.

A dying farm in the central valley of California lies smothered in white mineral salts. This crop-killing residue gradually builds up as salt-laden waters are used to irrigate the region's fields. Drainage systems that maintain proper salt balance in the soil are being used successfully on some of the region's farms.

The once mighty Colorado River, reduced to a mere trickle by damming and diversion to water the parched Southwest, peters out on a creek bed in Mexico, still 30 miles short of its mouth in the Gulf of California.

1895. The dam blocks the flow of the river, raising its level to establish an artificial fall. The dam backs up the river's water into a reservoir, or artificial lake, that fills up during periods of high river flow. The water is stored there, like energy in a storage battery, and then released when called upon to do work.

Flowing on demand, water from the reservoir plummets down through big conduits, or penstocks, to the power station below. There, turbines— essentially refined water wheels with curved vanes that are turned by the flow—convert the kinetic energy of the moving water into mechanical energy. The turbine spins the rotor of a generator, which changes the mechanical energy into electricity.

In recent years, the high cost of big dams and increasing environmental concerns have brought a renewed interest in small-scale power development. Such projects include the mounting of turbines in free-flowing streams without use of dams or reservoirs, as well as the revitalization of old and abandoned small dams. Since 1968 more than 90,000 small hydro plants have been built in China alone.

Even the United States, which uses more power than any other nation, had a fruitful field for expansion in building small-scale hydro plants. Hydrologists have calculated that the rivers in the United States carry an average flow of about two million cubic feet of water per second down an average vertical distance of 1,650 feet. These falling waters represent a theoretical energy potential of 300 million horsepower, more than enough to meet present U.S. requirements for electricity.

Despite the smaller-is-better trend, gargantuan hydro projects are still being constructed. The Grand Coulee Dam, the world's largest until 1981, was supplanted that year by the Itaipu Dam (*pages 72-77*), on the Paraná River between Paraguay and Brazil. The Itaipu Dam will soon be surpassed by other dams now in the early stages of construction. The largest of these is under development in the remote sub-Arctic wilderness of northern Quebec, where wintertime temperatures often drop to −40° F.

Construction of the $15 billion project began in 1971. Centered on La Grande Rivière between Labrador and James Bay, it calls for nothing less than the topographic rearrangement of a 68,000-square-mile region, larger than all of England. Through construction of hundreds of miles of rock-and-earth dikes and dams standing up to 50 stories high, the flow of three big rivers is being rechanneled and routed into the La Grande complex. The La Grande will then bulge into a series of 198 dikes, eight main dams and five major reservoirs storing water for three power stations.

The first generators, using energy supplied by water falling 590 feet through tunnels, went on line in 1979. By the year 2000, when the project is scheduled for completion, five main power stations powered by 60 turbines will produce 13,900 megawatts of electricity—enough to serve more than 10 million homes.

While such projects will bring unquestionable material advantages as well as protection from floods and other side benefits, large-scale tampering with the natural work of a river almost always produces unexpected or unwanted consequences. In addition to the obvious result of endangering the habitats of fish and other aquatic organisms, man-made alterations can disrupt the river's normal patterns of erosion and deposition.

When the river reaches the still water of a reservoir, for example, it slows

At the largest of three power stations in Quebec's La Grande Rivière hydroelectric complex, the overflow from a 1,134-square-mile reservoir foams down a spillway of 10 gigantic stairs. The steps, each 33 feet high by 445 feet wide, were designed to slow the torrent of water and thereby minimize downstream erosion.

down suddenly and dumps practically all of its sediments. In silt-heavy regions, the reservoir may fill up with sediments and thus be rendered useless in as brief a period as 20 years. And there may be dramatic after-effects well downstream. Water released by the dam is virtually clear and thus able to scour with renewed energy certain downriver areas not formerly subject to severe erosion.

Even more complex changes in the sequence of erosion and deposition have been set in motion by the construction of Egypt's Aswan High Dam during the 1960s. The dam's 2,000-square-mile reservoir, Lake Nasser, traps much of the silt that formerly enriched the flood plain and delta; to compensate, farmers now must apply large quantities of costly chemical fertilizers to their land. At the same time, the dam and reservoir have tipped the delicate balance of delta building. Deprived of the constant addition of sediment from upstream, the Nile delta is now losing ground to wave erosion by the Mediterranean Sea.

Just as rivers constantly reshape their own channels, they constantly make adjustments to compensate for human intervention. When human beings build a dam to create a reservoir or dredge a channel to improve navigation, the river reacts to restore its most effective balance. Yet the damage may never be undone.

Ultimately, the challenge to hydrologists and engineers is not to stop building dams or refining a river's channel but to understand better the behavior of running water. "One should instigate those changes closest to the natural ones and seek to disturb the river equilibrium as little as possible," writes Kenneth J. Gregory, the eminent English geographer. "It is for this reason that river engineers in the United States and elsewhere have adopted the motto of 'working with the river rather than against it.' " Ω

Flowing through a diversion channel 500 feet
wide and more than a mile long, the Paraná River snakes around the nearly completed main
dam in a photograph that was taken in 1981. At
left, on the Paraguayan side of the river,
stand a wing dam and spillway.

BUILDING THE BIGGEST DAM

"At the foot of the main dam, all is bustle," wrote a visitor in 1982, when the Itaipu Dam was nearing completion on the Paraná River between Brazil and Paraguay. "But on top of the dam — 62 stories high and 4.8 miles long — there are no machines and no people, and the only noise is the wind racing across the vast artificial lake, which is spreading north as far as the eye can see."

The visitor was describing the most ambitious engineering feat of its kind ever undertaken. The Itaipu Dam, which became the world's largest hydroelectric installation when the first of its 18 mammoth generators went on-line in 1983, is an epic enterprise by every measure. It cost 13 billion dollars and involved as many as 24,000 on-site workers. The commission in charge of the joint Brazilian-Paraguayan project built several plants to process needed materials, along with 9,500 housing units, four hospitals, a school system for 15,700 pupils and enough restaurants to serve 770,000 meals a month.

Work on the dam itself began in 1975. To build the main dam and the huge powerhouse, work crews diverted the Paraná from its normal bed into an immense trough that detoured the construction site. Much of the excavated debris was later used in the project's 15.7 million cubic yards of concrete — enough material to build eight medium-sized cities. The whole gigantic endeavor will come to fruition in 1989, when the dam is to begin operating at maximum capacity, generating 75 billion kilowatt-hours a year.

The project has not been without attendant problems. Thousands of farm families were evicted from lands to be flooded by the artificial lake. The lake has made the local climate windier and cooler and a potential threat to the area's cash crops of wheat and coffee beans.

Yet the dam has produced an enormous net gain. A member of the binational commission summed up: "Itaipu is generating vast quantities of clean and renewable energy. It is creating thousands of jobs for Brazilian and Paraguayan workers. The magnificent artificial lake will supply water for drinking and irrigation." The dam is expected to last 50 to 200 years. After that, "Itaipu could be opened up," said a project director, "and the Paraná would flow in the same way it did before."

In a picture taken after the diversion channel was closed in 1982, the Paraná River fills an 870-square-mile reservoir above the dam. The river has returned to its normal channel, generating power by rushing through penstocks — S-shaped tubes — and dropping 396 feet.

Tier upon tier of concrete blocks rises to form the colossal main dam and the powerhouse built into its base. The millions of cubic yards of concrete needed to complete the job would have been costly and time-consuming to import. Instead, the builders erected their own on-site cement plant (*inset*), lopping an estimated 10 years off Itaipu's construction schedule.

The interior of Itaipu's cavernous power-house, 3,100 feet long and 367 feet high, nears completion in these pictures. At left, a huge section of a cylindrical steel pipe is moved into position; the finished conduit will deliver nearly 1,000 cubic yards of water per second to one of the turbines, which are spaced at intervals of about 110 feet. To dramatize the immensity of the turbines, the manufacturer had a symphony orchestra perform inside one of them before it was delivered to the dam site.

Chapter 3

THE LIVING STREAM

Y̶ou cannot step twice in the same river," Heraclitus wrote 2,500 years ago, "for fresh waters are ever flowing upon you."

With his intellectual passion for pointing out apparent opposites in nature and then finding connections between them, the Greek philosopher put his finger on the essence of the river: Its water is forever in motion.

This simple fact of flowing water, which still inspires poets and intrigues scientists, profoundly influences the ecology of the river. Unlike the still water of a lake, where the same water must be recycled again and again, running water is constantly being renewed, creating a more dynamic environment for living organisms.

This lotic environment — flowing water — affects the evolution of river life in myriad ways. Running water constantly replenishes the supply of oxygen, carbon dioxide and nutrients. In addition, it sometimes speeds the metabolism of aquatic organisms. For example, laboratory studies have shown that mayfly nymphs in rivers consume more oxygen than similar species in lakes. Even plant life is more active metabolically. One species of stream algae not only respires more rapidly than its lake counterpart but also absorbs the nutrient phosphorus at a rate up to 10 times as fast.

Running water creates a wide variety of biological niches, each one home to specially adapted flora and fauna. By flowing at different speeds, it provides different environments for fish species and for the many families of insects whose immature aquatic stages play a key role in stream ecology. And by reshaping the stream through erosion and deposition of sediments, running water furnishes diverse habitats — bare rock, cobbles, gravel, sand, silt or mud — for organisms that live on or beneath the stream bed.

Largely as a result, the stream is richer in life-forms than the still waters of lakes. Rivers are abiding evolutionary havens for virtually all taxonomic groups of fresh-water animal life. Rare is the aquatic organism not found there. Nearly all species of fresh-water fish — including most of the 2,000 species of minnow, the largest family of fish — live in running water. Insects, too, reach maximum variety in flowing water. In fact, the young of the insect family Simuliidae, which consists of no fewer than 300 species of biting blackflies, exist only in swift currents.

The task of interpreting this richness and diversity presents an extraordinary challenge to limnologists. Wading into the running water with their nets and hip boots, they already have learned a great deal about the ecology of little creeks and small rivers in the earth's temperate regions. Less is known about large river systems such as the Amazon, but investigators

A Eurasian kingfisher extends its wings to brake an unsuccessful dive for a fish. The bird, which may make more than 100 such plunges in a single day, is one of the countless shore-dwelling species that depend almost exclusively on aquatic life for food.

79

A mountain stream races over shallow riffles and deep pools in Waterton Lakes National Park in Alberta, Canada. The turbulent, oxygen-rich riffles are the primary residences of the myriad invertebrates and single-celled plants that form the basis of the rivers' food chain.

have started to make inroads in even these complex tropical ecosystems.

The velocity of water is only one of several environmental factors shaping stream life; other characteristics such as water temperature, water chemistry and stream-bottom material (substrate) also play an important role. But the speed of the current is the common denominator. It provides an element of unity for otherwise diverse communities of plants and animals, linking them, as a German limnologist put it, like "pearls on a string."

All of the factors that determine the speed of running water — slope, width, depth and stream-bed roughness — can produce variations in velocity and biological habitats over the length of one river. But even a single stretch of the stream has parcels of water moving at different speeds. The current is faster in the middle of the stream, away from the frictional drag exerted by the banks. It is also faster just below the surface. Velocity then decreases with depth under the influence of stream-bed friction.

The relatively tame water at the stream bottom is home to numerous species of insect larvae and nymphs and to other invertebrates such as mollusks. These benthic, or bottom-dwelling, creatures find refuge here from the turbulence of faster-moving waters. A favorite habitat of other creatures is the bed of a riffle, a shallow area of turbulent water passing through or over gravel and large rocks. So many invertebrates inhabit the riffle that it has been termed "the larder of the lotic environment."

Life can flourish there in part because of the boundary layer, a thin layer of water above the stream bed where friction virtually stops the current. Limnologists long had suspected the existence of the boundary layer, but they had never actually been able to measure it in a river. A single uneven rock in the stream bed can produce complex microcurrents that prevent reliable measurements of stream velocity.

In the early 1950s, however, a Swiss biologist devised an ingenious experiment to demonstrate and to measure this boundary layer of virtually motionless water. In a laboratory, Heinz Ambühl created a minuscule artificial river with flowing water, a stone-studded stream bed and a glass bank for observation. In order to make visible the currents along the bottom in his cross section of river, Ambühl released tiny particles of acetyl cellulose into the flowing water and photographed them. They showed up as dotted streaks in the photographs. Where the current was slowest around the stones of the stream bed, the white dots clustered most closely. Ambühl's photographs revealed the boundary layer: Just above a stone was a zone of water about one tenth of an inch thick that was nearly motionless.

Evolution has tailored many tiny organisms to squeeze into the boundary layer. Stoneflies and mayflies possess flattened bodies that provide them with a low profile. Other species are equipped with special anatomical devices such as hooks, grapples, suckers or friction pads that enable them to cling to stones and thus remain in the slack current of the boundary layer without being swept downstream.

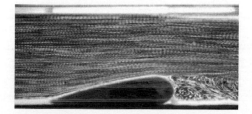

This laboratory photograph, taken in 1955 by Swiss researcher Heinz Ambühl, documents the existence of a motionless boundary layer that covers objects in the stream bed and protects invertebrates from the current. The boundary layer appears as a solid line, while the moving water — flowing from left to right — is marked by streaks and eddies.

Outside the boundary layer, many nymphs and larvae show a distinct preference for a certain range of current velocity. In many cases, researchers can accurately predict which species will be found at a given speed — and where. After an intensive study of Rattlesnake Creek in Montana, biologist Joseph P. Linduska discovered that when he knew the current velocity, he could forecast the location on a submerged boulder of 11 kinds of mayfly nymphs. If the current changed, the mayflies moved to new positions.

Other insects demonstrate their preferred current speeds in a different manner. Many species of the major order Trichoptera, or caddis flies, have larvae that build movable protective cases of sand grains, pebbles, plant stems and other materials from the stream bed. Species using lightweight construction materials generally live in areas of least current, while those building with good-sized pebbles live in swifter water. Scientists studying caddis flies can observe this adaptive mechanism. If a larva is removed from its case and the surrounding current is artificially speeded up, it often will select larger, heavier materials for building a new mobile home.

The insects perhaps best equipped for life in running water belong to the family Simuliidae; the larvae anchor themselves in swift currents and make use of the flow to bring them food. Popularly known as blackflies ("buffalo gnats" in North America, because of their humpbacked appearance), these little insects, only about one tenth of an inch long as adults, are among the most widely distributed of the creatures that spend part of their lives in streams. They are also among the most dreaded, for the adult females are fierce bloodsuckers. Female blackflies need protein from a blood meal in order for their eggs to develop, and they take it wherever they can, using their piercing mouthparts to attack deer, birds, livestock and humans.

Nearly two centuries ago, the great German explorer Alexander von Humboldt encountered swarms of vicious blackflies in South America at the Great Cataracts, where the Orinoco River plunges over a series of rocky sills. "I doubt whether there is a country on earth where man is exposed to more cruel torments in the rainy season," he wrote in 1800. "It is neither the dangers of navigating in small boats, nor the savage Indians, nor the serpents, crocodiles, or jaguars that make Spaniards dread a voyage on the Orinoco; it is, as they say, *el sudar y las moscas* (the sweat and the flies)."

Humboldt was not exaggerating. In certain river valleys of South America and tropical West Africa, blackflies transmit the parasitic filarial nematode, which afflicts up to 75 per cent of the human populations with a disease called onchocerciasis, or river blindness. In addition to causing partial or total blindness, this disease can lead to disintegration of the skin's normal structure with an effect that, in the words of a doctor working in the Sudan, "makes young people look old and old people look like lizards."

Largely because blackflies carry dangerous parasites, they have been the subject of scores of studies in the wild and in laboratories. Biologists have created indoors the running-water habitat Simuliidae needs, sustaining the insects through complete life cycles by giving adult females warmed cow blood inside easily punctured chicken-skin pouches. Consequently, the lives of blackflies are among the best known of river creatures.

In the wild, many blackfly species produce two or more generations each year. Females lay eggs on rocks, logs or vegetation at the water's edge. Some lay their eggs one at a time while flying over the surface with the tip of their abdomen in the water; the eggs that survive predation and the current slowly settle to the bottom. The eggs of some species hatch quickly; others winter in the stream and hatch under the stimulus of warming water. When the eggs hatch, the larvae move to rock surfaces where the current is swift, often in such numbers that the mass resembles black moss.

Some blackfly species attach themselves not only to rocks but to other aquatic animals. The discovery of this habit lay at the heart of a fascinating biological detective story enacted in East Africa during the 1940s.

The sleuth was a British biologist, John P. McMahon, and he was looking for the breeding place of the blackfly *Simuliim neavei,* a species known to carry the parasite that causes river blindness. McMahon assumed that the species bred in the Kipsonoi River or in one of its tributaries.

He searched all of the usual breeding places — stones, sticks, the riverbed itself, leaves, tree roots and trailing grasses in the water. Failing to find any *neavei* larvae, he next examined vegetation and wet places near the river. He even dammed up streams and diverted watercourses to dry up waterfalls and cascades so that their bottoms could be searched in great detail.

Though all these efforts failed, McMahon was certain he was on the right track. An application of DDT to fast-flowing rivers in western Kenya reduced the numbers of *neavei* adults — evidence that larvae had been present somewhere in the water. McMahon then learned about an instance, elsewhere in Africa, of blackfly larvae living on mayfly nymphs. He and his associates immediately began catching and examining invertebrates in tributaries of the Kipsonoi. Each day for three weeks they examined 2,000 insects, as well as fish and crabs, but they found no *neavei*.

McMahon concluded that some creature living in the main river, not in the tributaries, carried the blackfly. On the second day of hunting the river,

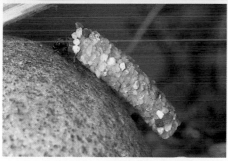

Masters of self-protection, stream-dwelling caddis-fly larvae construct elaborate cases as camouflage from predators and as ballast against the current. Soon after hatching *(top)*, a larva begins protecting itself with bits of material cemented together with silklike threads produced through a pore near its mouth. It uses whatever building materials are best suited to counteract the speed of the current: leaves, small shells, twigs or stream-bed gravel.

they found live *neavei* larvae on a crab *(Potamon niloticus)*. In fact, about half of the crabs they examined carried the blackflies on their backs.

Whether anchored to a crab or to a stone, blackfly larvae move about like a rock climber on a cliff face. A larva attaches itself to the surface with silk strands spun from its salivary glands. Then it weaves the strands into a silk mat with hooks on its front proleg, a fleshy appendage protruding from the abdominal segment. Bending its body sharply, the larva brings its rear proleg around to the mat so that its head can then let go and weave another mat in a new position. Repeating the process, the larva moves safely over surfaces swept by water. Like many spiders, it also attaches a silk safety cord to its rock so that, if dislodged, it can pull itself back upstream.

The blackfly larva collects food mainly by unfolding a fanlike appendage from its head. This apparatus, thrust up into the current, catches drifting bits of organic matter. The larva feeds and grows for two to three months, then transforms itself into a pupa.

When a larva pupates, it spins a silk case that remains attached to its rock surface. Just before emergence of the adult, gas forms between the pupal and adult cuticles, and the adult is enveloped by a glistening, gaseous film held by surface hairs of its body as it emerges. The adult rises quickly to the surface and takes flight. The female lives two to three weeks, the male about one week. After mating, males spend their dwindling days sipping plant nectar while the females seek blood.

While the bloodthirsty blackfly thrives by adapting to the swiftest currents, other invertebrates demonstrate an opposite kind of adaptation to flowing water. They make their home beneath the stream bed's surface. Here, water percolates through sand and gravel at rates of less than an inch per hour but in sufficient quantities to bring oxygen and food particles.

Many of these subterranean dwellers are insect nymphs and larvae that spend their early lives a few inches deep in the gravel. Later, they may burrow into the sand and gravel during a bottom-scouring flood or when a stream nearly dries up. But other creatures spend their entire lives there. These mites, copepods, ostracods, tardigrades and syncarids are river dwellers that never experience true running water; they are beneath it all.

This subterranean world has been called the hyporheos — from the Greek for "to flow under." The abundance of life uncovered there has surprised biologists, whose sampling methods had until recently only scratched the surface of the hyporheic zone. In 1977, for example, two Canadians, H. B. Noel Hynes and Lyse Godbout of the University of Waterloo, probed the bed of Salem Creek, a shallow stream in Ontario. They found more invertebrates two to six inches beneath the gravel than at the bed's interface with water. The hyporheic life varied seasonally; at its peak in October, it was three times as plentiful as at the stream-bed surface.

Other studies suggest that the hyporheos may extend much deeper than formerly suspected. In stream beds where the deposits of sand and gravel are sufficiently coarse to allow water to filter through, rich and varied animal communities have been uncovered more than three feet down.

The level at which an aquatic creature lives is only one of the effects of running water. Like many insects, different fish species have evolved in waters of great clarity or turbidity, and the anatomy and physiology of these species show adaptation to the conditions. Fish that have evolved in clear waters typically have large eyes and keen vision. By contrast, the minnow known as the sturgeon chub, which is native to turbid streams in the American Great Plains, glimpses its muddy world through small eyes that are partly shielded from sand and silt.

Other fish in sediment-laden streams of the Great Plains have developed special sensory organs that enable them to find their way through the murky waters. They possess more or larger sensors in their lateral-line system, the array of organs along the head and sides that help fish detect the current and changes in pressure.

One of the most unusual adaptations to water turbidity belongs to the family of mormyrids that inhabit Africa's Zaire River. Commonly known as knife fish because of their slim and elongated snouts, these fish perceive their world through an electrical sense. An organ in the tail generates a high-frequency alternating current, which sheathes the body in an electric field. Objects entering this field distort it, and these distortions are detected by sensors lining the surface of the knife fish's body.

The speed of the current has directly influenced the evolution of other fish. Some, like sculpins and darters, are adapted to avoid the current's full force: They hug the bottom, where the current is relatively slack. This behavior is helped by the position of their eyes, which are near the top of the head, and by sturdy pectoral fins, which serve as hydrofoils, guiding the current to press the fish closer to the substrate.

Some fish stay attached to the stream bed with sucker-like mouths. In the gyrinocheilids, which are native to torrential Asian rivers, this adaptation has resulted in a rerouting of the respiratory apparatus. Instead of taking in oxygenated water through their mouths, they receive it laterally through a substitute opening on the sides of their heads.

Fast-swimming fish, such as trout, handle the current with the aid of streamlined bodies. In general, the rounder a fish's cross section, the faster it swims. A study of four common European species showed that the pike-perch, with the roundest cross section of the four, also had the highest swimming speed, 44 inches per second; the perch, rudd and bream, each with a relatively flatter cross section, had successively lower speeds, ranging downward to the bream's 32 inches per second, or just a little faster than the average current of its river habitat. By contrast, several species of very round and streamlined trout may swim at speeds of 102 inches per second.

The top speed of a fish is invariably a little faster than the current in its habitat. This enables the fish to hold station against the flow and to flee upstream from danger. It also facilitates respiration. By facing into the current, fish need only to open their mouths to obtain sufficient oxygen.

But even strong swimmers generally must avoid the full force of the current. Fish tire easily, becoming weak and vulnerable, because lactic acid builds up rapidly in their tissues (as much as eight times faster than in humans) and diminishes only slowly. As a result, they seek shelter in the dead water of eddies created on the downstream side of obstacles such as boulders, logs or sandbars. Skilled fishermen know that the best place to hook a trout is just downstream from an obstacle, and the bigger the obstacle, the bigger the potential catch. Once a big fish is hooked, the angler plays his catch back and forth in the stream in order to force the build-up of lactic acid in the exhausted fish and thus make it easier to land.

After a fast swimmer finds suitable shelter in slack water, it may spend

Ingenious Adaptations to the Current

The smallest aquatic animals often survive with ease in rivers whose fastest currents are strong enough to dislodge them from their habitat. Many tiny animals simply avoid the current. Aided by their small size, some settle down in the shelter of aquatic plants. Others dwell in the narrow belt of tranquility surrounding stream-bed rocks or burrow directly into the stream bed.

Many species have made physical adaptations. Some of them have evolved flattened shapes that present low profiles to the current. Other species have developed specialized equipment for survival, such as claws, suckers and glands that produce sticky secretions.

Some of the little animals instinctively choose the best environment. For example, a stonefly species will cling to the largest, most stable particles available. But many aquatic creatures choose the specific places and conditions for which evolution has prepared them. Those equipped with suckers will cling to smooth rocks, while clawed species invariably select the rough surfaces best suited to their physical nature.

The mayfly (*upper right*) and stonefly (*center*) nymphs have evolved streamlined shapes and clawed legs. The mayfly aims its broad, flattened head upstream to reduce the drag of the current. The stonefly's low profile permits it to reside in the narrow, tranquil boundary layer surrounding stream-bed objects.

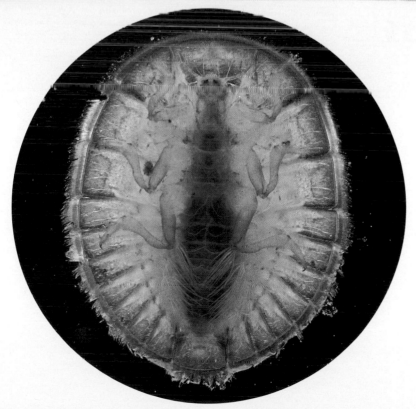

The water penny, or riffle-beetle larva, depends for security on six grasping legs and a flattened shell edged with tiny spines that seal it firmly to rough surfaces. The dual protection permits one species of water penny to withstand the torrents at the edge of Niagara Falls.

A back swimmer (*right*) uses its powerful, ▶
fringed hind legs as oars to propel it just below
the surface of quieter river regions. Buoyed
by air pockets along its ventral surface and guid-
ed by its keel-shaped back, it glides upside
down through the water, awaiting insect prey.

Denizen of the river bottom, a sculpin makes
do without the air-filled swim bladder that
buoys fish. To avoid being swept away, the
sculpin braces its strong, oversized pectoral fins
against the upstream sides of rocks and lets
the force of the current lock it safely in place.

A fresh-water mussel buries itself in the riverbed
and uses its bristled siphon to ingest water
and filter out microscopic food particles. By extending and retracting its single muscular foot,
the bivalve can inch along the river bottom.

An ostracod opens its bean-shaped shells and ▶
moves through the water by waving feelers, partially visible to the left of its shells. Only .04
inch in size, it generally resides amid the moss
that covers rocks near riffles; the moss protects it from the riffles' turbulent water.

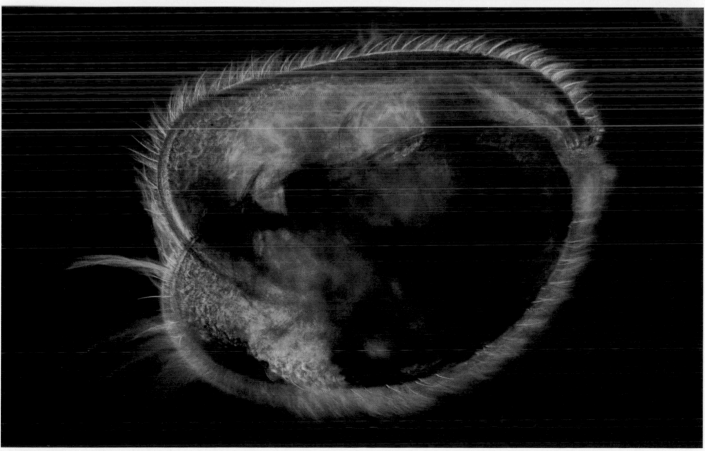

much of its time there. Species such as trout, salmon, dace and darters defend their respective parcels of stream bed, especially the slack-water spaces, by chasing intruders and snapping at them. This behavior accounts in part for the low survival rate of hatchery-reared trout that are released in streams. Resident fish dominate the newcomers, which may be continually rejected from occupied territories until they die of exhaustion.

In addition to its effects on the physical forms and habitats of fish, running water has also helped shape their reproductive behavior. Successful reproduction usually depends upon the current to keep renewing the supply of oxygen. Though a few species such as the shad lay semibuoyant eggs that drift until they hatch, most fish must find spawning places on the stream bed that serve a dual function: offering protection from the force of the water and from predators while still ensuring a supply of oxygen.

The problem is acute with a stream bed of mud or silt, which block the flow of oxygenated water with caked-together particles. Some species avoid caked stream beds by attaching their fertilized eggs to river vegetation or even to land plants that are covered by water during spring floods.

To escape muddy waters, some fish try to reach a stretch of rocks and gravel, where turbulent flow through the loose substrate ensures a continuous bath of oxygen for the eggs. A great many fish simply spawn over gravel, where the fertilized eggs settle into crevices. Darters, sculpins and some minnows lay eggs in natural openings beneath large stones. In California's San Joaquin River, biologists found nests of the prickly sculpin and the three-spined stickleback inside discarded beverage cans.

Nest-building species employ various methods to guarantee an adequate flow of oxygenated water. Many kinds of fish build nests that protrude above the stream bed. The fallfish—a minnow that grows to 18 inches in length—constructs its high nest by transporting stones in its mouth. The stones, which may be as much as three inches in diameter, are arranged in a pile up to two feet tall and six feet in diameter.

Other fish dig pits for their nests, using an ingenious variety of excavation techniques. The stone-roller minnow was named for its unusual method of construction. Males of the species push stones to a chosen site with their snouts or carry pebbles there with their mouths. Sometimes dozens of males work on a single large pit while females wait nearby. Then, one by one, they swim into the pit. A single male and female may mate, or several males may try to press against a female's sides—the act that stimulates her to release eggs. Only then do the males squirt out milt. Stone-roller eggs, heavy for their size, quickly fall into crevices among the stones of the pit.

Several species dig with their tails. The eel-like lamprey clears a nest in small gravel by fanning its tail. Female trout and salmon vigorously flap their tails so that stones are lifted off the bottom by negative pressure and then carried downstream by the current. When a suitable pit, or redd, is formed, its maker and a male spawn. The female then swims upstream a bit and dislodges stones that cover and protect the just-fertilized eggs.

Pit-diggers select well-aerated sites among stones and gravel. Biologists have observed that Atlantic salmon, brown trout and rainbow trout usually dig their nests at the downstream end of pools—where water enters a riffle and there is a downflow of water into the gravel. Brook trout tend to dig nests at the bottom of riffles, where water is deflected up through gravel.

The chub solves the problem of protection from the current by combin-

A paddlefish is specially equipped with a long, cartilaginous snout, which incorporates sensory organs for detecting food. The fish may use its snout to probe the river bottom for concentrations of plankton.

Piranhas display an oval shape and flattened sides, which permit nimble maneuvering in shallow water. Despite their bloodthirsty reputation, they live chiefly on dead or sick fish; rarely does a whole school attack in a feeding frenzy.

ing the two main methods of nest-building. First it digs a pit, excavating sand and stones that might stifle the supply of oxygenated water; then it constructs in the excavation a pile of stones through which the oxygenated water can freely flow.

Much of what is known about the labors of the chub stems from the studies conducted early in this century by biologist Jacob Reighard. Setting out to learn the nest-building behavior of chubs in a tributary of Michigan's Huron River, Reighard soon learned that his research would require binoculars, patience and stealth. Every time he approached the stream bank, the chubs would dart away from their nest-building work, which took place between mid-April and the end of May. "I often crept on hands and knees and again stopped for a time, with my head lifted only high enough to enable me to see the nest," Reighard wrote. "So by several stages I advanced stealthily until I was on the edge of the bank, and the fish were little, if at all, disturbed." In fact, the chubs soon ignored his presence.

Reighard took detailed notes about the nest-building of one male chub. First it cleared a circular pit, seizing "any projecting part of a stone that he can get into his mouth, at times jerking it from side to side to loosen it." The chub carried stones twice as big as its head. Larger ones were pushed along the bottom. The fish also picked up sand and gravel in its mouth, then spit it out away from the nest site. Once the pit was dug, the chub began filling the hole with stones, mostly brought from upstream. It even carried in dead and live mussels and a six-inch-long sheep bone. When the male chub's work was completed, the nest pile stood seven and a half inches high and more than three feet across.

Reighard waded into the creek and carefully undid the chub's work in order to count the stones and pebbles. There were about 7,050 of them, weighing a total of 88 pounds in water (235 pounds in air). A single six-inch-long river chub had moved them all in less than 30 hours, spread out over four days, and it had traveled back and forth an estimated distance of 16 miles in the process.

Nor was that the full extent of the male chub's herculean labors. If Reighard had not dismantled the pile, the chub would have dug a small trough in the top of the nest, spawned there with a female, lugged more stones to fill the trough, then guarded the nest for about four days. This process exhausts elderly fish, and many die of exertion. Most young male fish survive to repeat their labor during the next nest-building season.

Of all the ways in which the flow of water influences river ecology, none is more important than its role in providing nourishment. Because of the current, riverine food chains differ radically from those of lakes. In most lakes, the food chain is built on plankton and consists mostly of microscopic algae and other plant life called phytoplankton and of tiny animals called zooplankton that graze on the drifting plants. But in rivers, plankton is relatively unimportant. Most streams flow too rapidly to allow the full development of planktonic cell division and growth.

The exceptions occur typically in large rivers or dammed-up stretches where the water moves slowly enough to allow plankton to reproduce. Researchers on the Blue Nile found that both phytoplankton and zooplankton there thrived in a 221-mile stretch of the river during several dry seasons when the flow was low and slow, allowing the water a travel time of about 40 days. In England's Thames River, where water takes six or seven days to run the river's length, a more limited planktonic population develops. Virtually none occurs in rivers where the travel time of water is a few days.

Some limnologists suspect that where river plankton exists, it may consist mostly of specially adapted species. These species would be capable of entering a resting stage and then of reproducing quickly once suspended in flowing water under favorable conditions.

Support for the idea comes from A.I. el Moghraby of the University of Khartoum, who studied zooplankton in the Blue Nile in 1977. He discovered that zooplankton disappears almost completely during the annual flood. Then, as the current slows, silt settles out, light penetrates and phytoplankton bloom and zooplankton once again appear throughout the river. Moghraby discovered direct evidence of a resting stage. Eggs and adults found in water and in bottom sediments were in a state of diapause, or quiescence. And he learned that at least one kind of zooplankton can survive in that state for a long time. Specimens of a species of *Macrothrix,* found in a 55-year-old mud wall, sprang to life when placed in water.

Though the current prevents plankton from developing in most streams, it helps supply stream dwellers with other provisions. One important food source in temperate streams and small rivers is attached algae. These algae, in contrast to the algal forms of floating phytoplankton, have adapted to flowing water by clinging to stones and other underwater surfaces. Many fish and invertebrates such as mayfly nymphs feed directly on the rock-

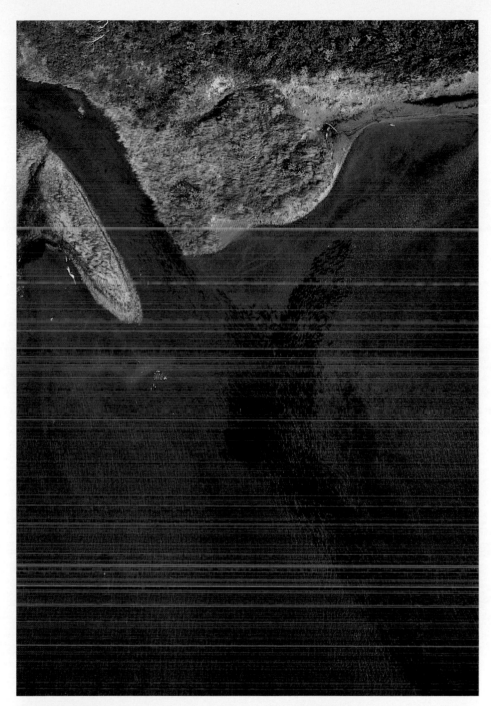

Thousands of sockeye salmon battle upstream through Alaska's Tazimina River system during their arduous return to native streams for autumn spawning. Many scientists believe that in the upstream struggle, the fish retrace the succession of strong olfactory impressions made by each body of water they passed through during their journey downstream to the sea.

A tiny salmon alevin, or hatchling, emerges from a pea-sized egg. The alevins, nourished by a yolk sac attached to their underside, will remain protected in their gravelly bed for several weeks, until ready to fend for themselves.

coating smorgasbord. Such higher organisms form a trophic group called grazers and scrapers, so called for their two different methods of removing the food from the rocks. They also dine on other aquatic plant life.

Other herbivores, which are known as collectors, simply wait downstream for a movable feast to arrive on the current. These passive feeders are equipped with an array of anatomical devices for filtering bits of plant life from the current. They may catch morsels with bristles on their legs or mouthparts. Or, like certain caddis-fly larvae, they may collect their food by spinning funnel-shaped nets.

The various particles of organic matter floating downstream are known to limnologists as detritus. The mixture consists not just of material grown in the stream but also of leaves, stems, flowers and fruits that grow on the river's shores and in its valleys. In fact, much of the food energy in the headwaters of most rivers comes from terrestrial sources. Without these nutrients, the river's upper stretches could support only a fraction of its abundant animal life. The fertility of a valley thus helps determine the richness of running water.

Organic matter is blown or washed into the stream or simply falls in from overhanging trees. A river is especially rich in food energy near its source; headwaters often flow through forests and receive more organic matter per unit area than broader downstream stretches. Some streams almost suffocate in the autumn as tons of dead leaves decay, depleting the supply of dissolved oxygen required for decomposition.

The process by which leaves and other terrestrial organic matter are converted into nutrients for aquatic animals begins with bacteria and fungi that already inhabit the leaves when they enter the water. Some of these microorganisms are adapted to adhere to leaves even in swirling currents. Moreover, many of the organisms, especially certain species of fungi, possess special enzymes to aid in plant decomposition. The enzyme cellulase, for example, breaks down the abundant cellulose of the plant cell. Fungi work best in flowing, well-oxygenated water; a leaf buried in sand or silt decays more slowly because the low supply of oxygen suppresses the growth of fungi.

After microbe-induced decomposition begins, the trophic group of invertebrates known as shredders start to work. Shredders, including crane-fly larvae and some caddis-fly larvae, stonefly nymphs and some crayfish, bite or tear the soft parts of the leaf between the veins, ingesting tiny fragments. Dead leaves in themselves are a fair source of nutrients. One analysis found them roughly equivalent to hay in nutritional value. Another showed elm leaves to contain 7.5 per cent of their air-dried weight in protein.

However, shredders are attracted not by the leaf but by the fungi and other microbes at work there. In laboratory experiments, shredders prefer the leaves that harbor the most fungi and thus decay most quickly — elm over maple, for example. They eat the leaves to get at the microbes. In limnologist Kenneth Cummins' analogy, the leaves are their "crackers" and the microbial tissue is what they really want — the "peanut butter."

It is estimated that shredders convert only 40 per cent of leaf matter to their own tissues and to carbon dioxide. The rest is passed as feces. Even this nutritional material is used: Many river creatures, including fish, practice coprophagy, or feces-eating.

The waste matter and uneaten particles of detritus float downstream with masses of tiny invertebrates. These organisms — snails, some worms, the

Mating Habits of the Stickleback

Animal behaviorists have long been fascinated by the mating habits of fish and by the instinctive ingenuity with which various species protect their nests and their young from predators and the river current. To avoid the difficulties of on-site study, researchers routinely bring specimen fish into laboratories, where experiments can easily be controlled and observed in tanks. A favorite subject for such studies is the three-spined stickleback, a four-inch-long fish common to the rivers of the Northern Hemisphere. Researchers prefer it because the stickleback is hardy in the laboratory, neurologically simple and especially interesting in its elaborate mating ritual.

The stickleback's reproductive cycle, shown in this sequence of photographs, begins each spring with a surge of hormones that makes the female fertile and produces striking physical changes in the male. In coloring, the male loses his mottled brown, grey and green tones, which make him virtually indistinguishable from the female; his underside turns red, his back a bluish white and his eyes become a bright blue.

With his new brilliance, the male becomes aggressive, attacking any males that venture near. This behavior is a simple reaction to the stimulus of seeing the color red on the males' bellies. In a confirming experiment, researchers found that when a male saw a red truck passing the laboratory window, he attacked the image as vigorously as he assaulted other males. And even as the male defends his territory, he undertakes the arduous work of nest building.

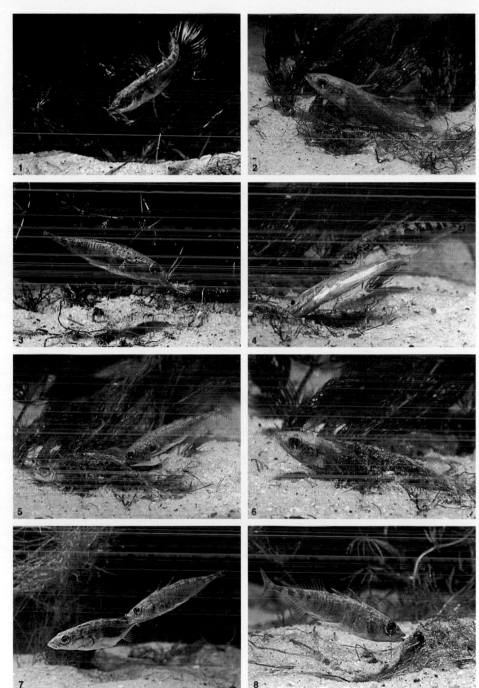

A male three-spined stickleback (1) carries plant material to his nest and (2) glues the nest with a secretion from his kidneys. Next (3), he adds sand to the tunnel-shaped nest for support and (4) entices a fertile female to enter. He nudges the female's tail (5), stimulating her to spawn 50 to 100 eggs; he then (6) fertilizes the eggs. Protecting them, he drives away his predatory mate (7) and (8) fans the nest frequently to supply the eggs with adequate oxygen until they hatch in 10 to 14 days.

aquatic young of insects — have been swept up from their habitats on the stream bed. Awaiting them are the carnivores, including some flesh-eating insects, such as the large stoneflies and caddis flies, but mostly fish, which need only to face the flow and open their mouths in order to dine.

This currentborne gift of prey is known as drift. Limnologists can measure drift by several methods, most simply by suspending a fine-mesh net across a stream. From such samples under a bridge on the Missouri River, a pioneer in the study of drift, Lewis M. Berner, calculated that 64 million tiny animals, weighing 440 pounds, passed by in one 24-hour period.

Drift follows a steady pattern. It increases at night, just after sunset, but not during full moonlight. The predilection of many insects to drift during

A quarter-inch-long blackfly larva, clinging to a blade of grass with tiny hooks and suckers, extends its fan-shaped mouth brushes to filter microscopic particles of food from circulating water. Blackfly larvae can also spin a strand around some stable object, and if they are swept away, they can make their way back by reeling in the strand.

darkness probably stems from the predatory habits of certain fish. Several studies have shown that the largest aquatic nymphs and larvae drift more at night than during the day, and that moonlight suppresses the drift of big individuals more than that of smaller ones. This pattern seems to be a response to fish predation. Both brook and rainbow trout are known to prefer large insects, and trout select their prey by sight, which is limited at night except in full moonlight.

Some bottom-dwellers apparently join the drift as a part of their reproductive behavior. The streamborne population of the shrimplike *Gammarus pulex* reaches its maximum during breeding season, an indication its movement may be related to mate-finding or some other aspect of reproduction.

Competition for food and living space also causes some invertebrates to catch a ride on the current and disperse downstream. This fact would account for the speed with which newly cut channels, or parts of rivers that have been cleared of all life by the heat from installations such as power plants, are quickly repopulated by drift from upstream.

Biologists trying to understand drift have traced its development back to the very sources of streams. Thomas Waters found in southeastern Minnesota an ideal place to study the beginnings of drift. There, a stream called South Branch Creek originates in a cave. At the cave mouth and at intervals downstream, biologist Waters set up drift-catching devices. Nothing drifted from the cave. But at the very first station, just 50 feet downstream, the stream was already carrying significant numbers of mayflies, caddis flies and midges. And Waters found that all these groups reached their maximum densities within a distance of 250 feet from the cave.

Since drift moves only downstream, the question naturally arises: How did these insect groups colonize the stream bed within a short distance of the stream's source at the cave mouth? The answer lies in some compensatory behavior of bottom-dwelling animals. Adult female mayflies, blackflies, caddis flies and stoneflies have all been observed flying upriver, where they lay eggs. Moreover, some insect nymphs actually make their way upstream against the current. Such movements of one mayfly species have been measured in Canada. Traveling along the stream bed at a rate of more than 200 yards a day, this insect moved a full mile upstream.

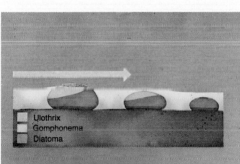

This drawing, based on research by noted botanist John L. Blum, shows that certain algae grow selectively on river rocks. On the stone that breaks the turbulent surface, Ulothrix grows in a narrow band that extends to the surface on the upstream side. Just below on the same stone are bands of Gomphonema and Diatoma. Gomphonema and Diatoma also appear on the submerged second stone, washed by fast-flowing waters, and Diatoma alone grows on the third and smallest stone, located in slower water. Each type of alga grows best on the upstream side of stones, where the moving water supplies essential nutrients.

Limnologists have worked out the details of the lotic food chain, from algae and fungi through predator fish, principally by studying small streams in the temperate regions. In recent years, however, they have extended their investigations to include large tropical rivers such as the Amazon, the mightiest on earth.

The Amazon is fabulously rich in fish fauna. In its 4,000-mile length from the Peruvian Andes to the Atlantic, 1,300 species have been recorded — more than in any other river. By contrast, the Mississippi harbors only 250 species of fish. Indeed, as the Swiss naturalist Louis Agassiz noted more than a century ago, the Amazon contains more kinds of fish than does the entire Atlantic Ocean from Pole to Pole. For people who live along the Amazon, the fish are often the only source of protein.

For many years, the Amazon's multitude of fish species mystified limnologists. They knew that the river's richness could be attributed in part to its basin's diverse habitats and to its more than 60 million years of evolutionary history. Many food chains can be traced to so-called floating meadows of such plants as water lettuce, water hyacinth and semiterrestrial grasses. These meadows develop near shores in calm stretches of the river and in lakes that fill up when the Amazon overflows and inundates its flood plain every spring. Many invertebrates feed on these meadows: Up to 700,000 have been counted within 11 square feet of meadow.

Yet these lush habitats, the most productive in all the Amazonian waters, are exceptions. Astonishingly, the Amazon itself is widely lacking in the dissolved nutrients needed to support the kind of food chains required by so many species of fish. In effect, the river is impoverished by the rich rain forests bordering its banks. In these forests, which represent the thickest plant growth on earth, dead vegetation quickly decomposes in the tropical heat, and the resulting nutrients are almost immediately absorbed by the greedy roots of the forest. Consequently, in more than 98 per cent of the Amazon basin, the soil that leaches in the water is nutrient-poor.

Some tributaries, known as black rivers, are dark brown from humic acids draining from forest soils. Other tributaries, so-called white rivers, are ocher-colored from loamy sediments and neutral or alkaline in pH. But both types are so poor in nutrients that they have been likened to "distilled water a little bit contaminated." Indeed, the acidic black streams are so nutrient-poor that they are known locally as "rivers of starvation."

There was no easy explanation for the paradox of the Amazon's amazing abundance of fish species in the midst of its apparent poverty of nutrients. The answer was finally supplied in 1976 by Belgian researcher Georges Marlier. After analyzing the stomach contents of numerous Amazonian fish, Marlier concluded: "These fishes are found to feed frequently on items which are derived not from the aquatic biological cycle but from the terrestrial environment of these waters, i.e., from shore forest. Many species feed directly on leaves, seeds, fruits or on terrestrial insects or other invertebrates which take their subsistence in the riparian vegetation. It is thus the forest which maintains the fish fauna at its present high level."

Subsequent research has supported these findings and shown that seasonal floodings facilitate the process. For example, when a major tributary, the Madeira River, overflowed its banks, researchers followed a stream of floodwater far into the forest. There they observed fish dining on leaves, fruits, seeds and practically any other plant matter that fell into the water.

In a sense, the research merely confirms what fishermen of the Amazon basin have known all along. They often use fruit as bait, and different fish species have their own favorite kinds. Fishermen sometimes wait with bow and arrow in canoes near overhanging laurel-like fruit bushes called uaracú-tamacoarí, then shoot the fish as they rise to catch fruits that drop and float on the surface. Another strategy is to attract fish by striking the water surface with fishing rods in imitation of falling fruit. Fishermen have even learned to mimic the sound of exploding seed pods of one flood-plain plant, a noise that usually brings a swarm of hungry fish.

The fish that eat terrestrial organic matter also help perpetuate plant life. Investigation of 33 species of flood-plain trees and shrubs shows that about half produce seeds or fruits that pass intact through the digestive tracts of fish; when the fish defecate, they unwittingly serve as dispersal agents for the plants. The seeds wash ashore and take root, and eventually the plant provides seeds or fruit for future generations of fish.

Other creatures help enrich the Amazon's impoverished water in much the same way the fish do. Most remarkable are four species of the fearsome caimans — crocodilians that reach up to 15 feet in length.

The caiman's unusual role in river ecology has been closely studied by Ernst J. Fittkau of Germany's Max Planck Institute for Limnology, the principal center for Amazon research. Fittkau points out that enormous schools of certain fish migrate from the flood-plain lakes or from the Amazon itself to the so-called river-lakes — wide bulges in tributaries where the water is typically poor in dissolved nutrients. The fish spawn in the river-lakes and then leave their offspring to hatch.

The caimans take a predatory interest in all this activity. Caimans catch and eat many of the migrating fish. Then, in the process of defecation, these caimans add nutrients to the waters. Thus, in preying upon the migrating

Living in a strong current, water starwort (*light green*) and water crowfoot (*dark green*) manifest adaptations to their environment. The flexibility of such aquatic plants makes it possible for their stems to bend with the flow of the water while their long roots remain securely anchored to the stream bed.

parents, caimans actually help establish an increased food base for the young fish that hatch there.

During the 1940s, however, the population of caimans began to decline. Much valued for their tough, exotic hides, they were decimated by hunters time and again. Tanning factories in the northern Brazilian city of Manaus alone were reportedly processing five million black caiman skins a year.

As the caiman declined, so did the fish populations of the river-lakes. Few caimans were left to prey upon the spawning runs of fish and to deposit the nutrients that helped sustain life in the river-lakes. Finally, in 1971, caiman hunting was banned by law. But enforcement is difficult, and in the 1980s caimans were still regarded as endangered species.

The case of the caiman highlights the complex and often surprising linkages within the ecology of running water. Such studies have helped spur

Giant Amazon water lilies, buttressed by an
intricate web of veins and leaf tissue full of air
spaces, carpet a quiet Amazon River lake.
The leaves, which range upward in size to seven
feet across, offer habitat for birds, lizards,
ants, beetles and insect larvae.

A riverboat crosses into the silt-laden main
stream of the Amazon from the Rio Negro, a tributary darkened by humus from the surrounding forest floor. These two rivers continue
to flow parallel for approximately six miles
before their waters begin to merge.

efforts by limnologists and other scientists to limit the encroachments of
industry and agriculture in the Amazon basin. Their most immediate concern is wholesale cutting and burning of the rain forests, which do so much
to support the Amazon's wealth of fish species. Recent studies of satellite
photographs revealed that, in just one decade, 200,000 square miles of
forest had disappeared from the Amazon basin. An estimated 50,000 square
miles of forest are being cleared each year, principally to feed wood-pulp
mills and to provide open land for rice farming and cattle ranching.

Limnologists are beginning to understand how leaves, fruits and seeds
nurture the living stream. With help from national and international
organizations, they would be able to check and perhaps even reverse the
depletion of the Amazon basin. But they know that the future of the forests — and perhaps of the river ecosystem itself — is in jeopardy, and they
fear that help will come too late. Ω

EXOTIC CREATURES OF THE AMAZON

The animals of the Amazon River basin flourish in a benign yet demanding world where land and water overlap as in few other places on earth. The Amazon annually overflows 25,000 square miles of riverside forest and keeps the terrain flooded for half the year. The river itself is often poor in nutrients, but it flows past banks whose lush vegetation is a bountiful food source for both water and land animals. In adapting to these special conditions, various river creatures have come to differ from others of their kind in behavior and appearance.

Some of the region's land animals use physical features to avoid the floods. Among these are more species with prehensile tails than any other region can claim. Anteaters, porcupines, oposums, kinkajous (a distant relative of the raccoon) and of course monkeys — all rely on grasping tails for added security. On the other hand, several terrestrial species have adapted comfortably to the river. One is the capybara, a rodent that swims better than it walks.

Animals in the aquatic community have evolved a wide variety of special adaptations. With their heavy reliance on the land for food, numerous species of fish have developed molars for chewing the nuts and fruit that drop from the trees. Others have enlarged, specialized stomachs that permit them to build up a store of fat to use as needed when the water recedes. Many river creatures have developed supersensitive organs for navigating in waters so thick with silt that vision is drastically limited.

A remarkable mechanism has been evolved by a species of Amazon frog to protect its offspring from the river's strong current and from predators. The female frog carries her fertilized eggs embedded in the soft tissue of her back; the hatchlings pop out their heads and limbs but remain partially covered until they are fully developed and able to fend for themselves. In effect, this and other species have completely bypassed the tadpole stage, in which amphibians are particularly vulnerable to preying fish.

Such adaptations have ensured the survival of countless species in the flood plain of the Amazon. And, benefiting from the region's abundant supply of food, several of the species have grown to extraordinary size and weight. This largest of river basins is the home of the world's largest otters, largest freshwater turtles, largest eagles, largest rodents and snakes.

Extending its forelimbs, this Surinam toad, a species of frog, reaches out its finger-like projections in search of food. Special tactile sensors on the tip of each projection can locate a meal of aquatic animals in the murkiest waters.

A matamata's snorkel-like snout permits this turtle species to stay submerged for long periods, while its fringed neck and bumpy shell serve as camouflage. As unwary fish and crustaceans swim by, the turtle opens its huge mouth; water rushes in carrying the prey with it.

A boat-billed heron is a nocturnal feeder, and it rests quietly during the daytime. At dusk this heron begins wading through shallow water, using its broad, shovel-like bill to sift through the mud of the Amazon in search of small aquatic animals.

The world's most powerful bird of prey, the 10- to 20-pound harpy eagle is the terror of the Amazon rain forest. It has thick, immensely strong legs and talons, and easily carries off monkeys and sloths; yet it is swift and agile enough to capture parrots in full flight.

◄ The hoatzin is a strange bird in both habit and appearance. A clumsy flier, it takes wing with great difficulty and often crash-lands a few hundred feet away. The baby hoatzin *(inset)* is born with two claws on each wing and uses them as forelimbs to climb trees with agility within a few hours of birth. If it is threatened, the bird leaps from its nest into the river and swims to cover. When the danger has passed, the baby hoatzin pulls itself back to its nest with its clawed wings. Although the claws drop off as the bird approaches maturity, fully grown hoatzins continue to use their wings for climbing through foliage.

Two marbled hatchetfish, each less than two inches long, linger near the surface awaiting prey. The only true flying fish, members of the hatchetfish family flap their pectoral fins to propel themselves over the water; they can stay airborne for distances up to 16 feet.

The arapaima, which grows to 200 pounds and is one of the world's largest fresh-water fish, benefits from two adaptations. Its keen eyesight locates prey in murky waters, and its swim bladder serves as a primitive lung when the river's oxygen supply dwindles.

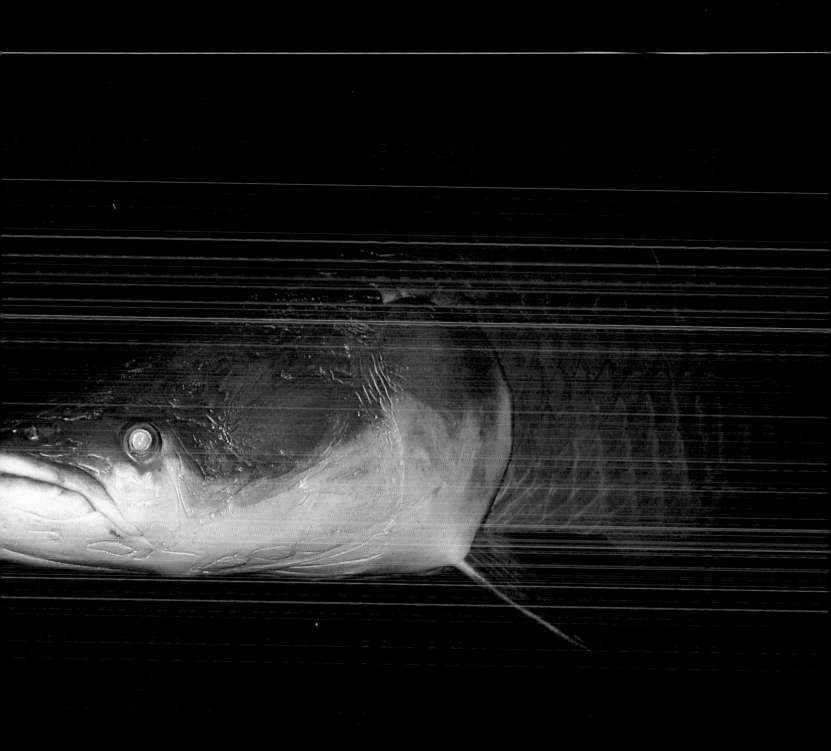

A herd of capybaras, the world's largest rodents, basks on a riverbank. These beasts, which generally weigh about 60 pounds and measure up to four feet in length, have molars that are specially modified to grind the mainstays of their diet — coarse grasses and aquatic plants.

The giant otter of the Amazon differs from other otters in having fully webbed forefeet. This feature, together with its standard flattened tail and webbed hind feet, makes the 60-pound animal a swift, nimble swimmer.

The Amazon dolphin, common throughout
the river basin, is believed to rely on a specialized snout, lined with a large number of sensory bristles, to locate fish in the murky water.
It shares with dolphins elsewhere a sophisticated system of navigating and finding food by
the echo of the sounds it emits.

The manatee has evolved small teeth with ridged grinding surfaces to chew its diet of tough, fibrous grasses. It has also developed a unique process of replacing worn teeth: New teeth regularly emerge in the back of the mouth as worn teeth move forward and finally fall out.

Chapter 4

THE LIFE CYCLE OF LAKES

Many students of nature have drawn inspiration from the beauty of a lake, but few have communicated their feelings as well as New England's philosopher-poet Henry David Thoreau. "Nothing so fair, so pure, and at the same time, so large as a lake, perchance, lies on the surface of the earth," he wrote. "Sky water."

The pool of sky water that Thoreau knew best was the one he made famous, Walden Pond. For two years during the 1840s, he lived in a crude hut on the shore of this little 64-acre lake near Concord, Massachusetts. Its waters sated his thirst— physiological and esthetic. At his every glance, the pond perfectly reflected the weather, so he called it "earth's liquid eye— it is blue or grey, or black as I choose my time." And he marveled at this "mirror no stone can crack."

The lakes Thoreau loved gave him a sense of permanence amid the fleeting affairs of men. But even as he tolled the seasons beside Walden Pond, the seemingly immutable body was changing, undergoing the slow aging that is the fate of all lakes.

Unlike rivers, which are long-lasting features of the landscape, lakes are ephemeral. Rivers endure; they serve as drains that remove wastes; their waters, always in a state of youthful renewal, carve new channels, ensuring survival. Lakes grow old; they serve as sinks that collect wastes; imprisoned in their own basins, they gradually fill up with sediment and become dry land. Scandinavia has tens of thousands of living lakes, but it has buried many, many more.

Some lakes come to a sudden end. In an extreme instance, the whole life cycle of a tiny beaver pond may consist of only a few days; a newly finished beaver dam gives way during a storm and the water flows out. The tectonic forces at work in the earth's crust can destroy a large lake's basin just as quickly as they shaped it. Though most lakes escape such catastrophes and survive for hundreds of thousands of years, even the deepest lakes live for only a tick or two of the earth's geological clock.

In the end, the life span of each lake is determined by a combination of circumstances and characteristics: the climate, the origin, size and shape of its basin, and above all the nature of the watershed—the area that the lake drains.

Early limnologists tended to look at lakes as independent phenomena and therefore to ignore their watersheds. They drew this conclusion from the American researcher Stephen Forbes, whose classic paper, published in 1887, decreed: "A lake is an old and relatively primitive system, isolated

Sutherland Falls, the highest waterfall in New Zealand, cascades 1,900 feet from Lake Quill into the Arthur River. The lake, which fills a cirque, or basin, gouged by glacial action, is the source of the river, though most lakes are collection points for rivers.

from its surroundings." Consideration of the lake thus stopped at the water's edge. "This was very natural," wrote Brian Moss, a contemporary English limnologist. "On one side you got your feet wet, on the other you did not!" But researchers soon began to realize that—as another limnologist put it—"a lake is more than just a basinful of water." They found that just as valleys greatly influence the streams that shaped them, so too the watershed has a lot to do with the life and death of a lake.

Though all lakes grow old in recognizable patterns, limnologists know best the life cycle of lakes in the populous, industrialized regions of the temperate zone, where their studies began. Once a temperate-zone lake has been formed, usually by glacial forces, life gradually takes shape in the new waters. A food chain forms, beginning at the bottom with microscopic plant life, extending upward to tiny animals and culminating with larger creatures that swim.

The foundation of the food chain in most lakes is the drifting algae known as phytoplankton—a word derived from the Greek for "plant" (*phyto*) and for "wanderer" (*plankton*). Some of these algae can actually swim, though just enough to maintain themselves at certain levels in the water; their wandering is powered by the lake currents. Various structural adaptations such as horns, spines and long sticklike bodies increase their surface area and thus help prevent phytoplankton from sinking.

Some lakes, like most rivers, fail to support substantial plankton populations because the water is discharged too rapidly, carrying away much of the algae before it can proliferate. In British Columbia's Marion Lake, for example, the water flows in from tributaries and exits through outlets so quickly that the entire volume of the lake is replaced in less than five days. The food chain has to depend largely upon plants rooted in the lake's shallow waters. By contrast, New Hampshire's Mirror Lake, which has less than one tenth the surface area of Marion Lake but is much deeper, renews its water only once a year and has grown a good crop of phytoplankton. California's Lake Tahoe is so deep that it requires 700 years for complete water renewal—but is so pure and nutrient-poor that its population of phytoplankton is relatively sparse.

The most common members of the phytoplankton community are diatoms, green algae and blue-green algae. These and other forms of free-floating algae are to lakes what grass is to the prairie: tiny chlorophyll factories for photosynthesis. Using the radiant energy of sunlight as their power, they convert the raw materials of carbon dioxide and dissolved mineral elements into the stuff of life—oxygen for respiration and cellular materials for consumption by organisms higher up the food chain.

Algal growth, and hence the productivity of a lake, depends in part upon the availability of at least 21 different mineral elements, including calcium, silicon and potassium. Minute amounts of certain minerals are carried in by rain and snow, and larger amounts come from the decay of lake organisms. But the principal source of these elements is the lake's watershed. The minerals leach from the soil and rocks underlying both the lake and the drainage areas of the inflowing tributaries. Where the terrain is dominated by granite or other hard and relatively insoluble rocks, the supply of nutrients eroded by the water will be scant and the lakes comparatively unproductive. The waters that erode sedimentary rocks and glacial deposits will carry far more nutrients.

Lake Williams, in the Cascade Range in Washington State, typifies the oligotrophic stage in a lake's normal aging process. Williams is a relatively young, clear body of water rich in dissolved oxygen. But the lake is poor in such nutrients as nitrogen and phosphorus, and therefore it is able to support only small colonies of plants and animals.

Two elements necessary for algal production are nitrogen and phosphorus, which are provided mainly by dissolved nitrate and phosphate salts. Phosphorus, the scarcer of the two elements, appears to be the key factor in algal production. This was dramatically demonstrated in an experiment conducted in a small Canadian lake in northwestern Ontario. The lake was selected because of its convenient violin-like shape. Across its narrow waist researchers stretched a vinyl-reinforced nylon curtain, which they sealed into the banks and into the mud at the bottom, effectively dividing the lake in two. They added to one side phosphate, nitrate and sucrose; the other side received only nitrate and sucrose. The phosphate-enriched side showed substantial increase in the growth of phytoplankton.

No less crucial to algal production is the amount of sunlight available for photosynthesis. Generally, the supply of year-round solar energy is highest in the tropics and lowest in the Arctic, with its long, dark winter. In temperate-zone lakes, foodmaking slows in winter but does not stop if sunlight penetrates the ice. Beneath the ice, small and motile algae concentrate at the top of the water where a little sunlight can penetrate. These algae are specially adapted to low light and cold water. Even in the permanently frozen lakes of Antarctica, enough light gets through the ice cover in summer to support specially adapted species of algae.

Sunlight and hence photosynthesis decrease sharply as the depth or turbidity of the water increases. In turbid waters, the light may penetrate only a few feet. By contrast, in an extraordinarily transparent lake such as Tahoe, sufficient light to support photosynthesis has been recorded at a depth of 300 feet. Except in waters shallow enough for sunlight to reach bottom, allowing the growth of rooted plants, lakes have two food-related layers: a food-generating upper zone, where light permits photosynthesis, and the dark lower zone, where no foodmaking can occur.

Sunlight affects algal production in another way: as a heating agent. This role hinges on the curious relation between water's temperature and density. Unlike other liquids, which are heaviest at the freezing point, water reaches its maximum density at about 39° F. Consequently, the densest water, which lies at the bottom of a lake, never freezes. If it were otherwise, a lake could freeze from the bottom up, destroying all its life in the process.

This relation between temperature and density results in a phenomenon called thermal stratification. During the warmest part of the year, practically all temperate-zone lakes exceeding 30 feet in depth become stratified in three distinct strata dictated by heat and hence by the density of the water.

In a typical temperate lake, thermal stratification closely follows seasonal changes in water temperature after breakup of the winter ice cover. In the early springtime, water temperatures and densities are nearly uniform at all levels. Because there is little thermal resistance to mixing, heat absorbed at the surface is easily blended into the lower levels of the lake by the action of the wind. The whole lake begins to warm.

Then, as the spring advances, the water near the surface heats rapidly and becomes lighter and more buoyant than deeper water. A temperature difference of a few degrees creates a barrier of thermal resistance, and complete mixing of the lake water stops. Thereafter, throughout the summer, the water is divided into three layers: the topmost epilimnion, where the water is warm, somewhat turbulent, well mixed; the middle metalimnion (or thermocline), a transition zone in which temperatures drop sharply with depth; and the bottom hypolimnion, where the water is cold and relatively undisturbed.

In the autumn, thermal stratification ends. As heat is lost to the atmosphere, temperature drops in the topmost epilimnion; density there increases and strong winds can once again mix waters freely from top to bottom. The lake's temperature then becomes nearly uniform, though higher than in the spring.

Stratification has great significance for algal production because it tends to block the circulation of nutrients across the thermal barriers between the layers. Nutrients from decaying organisms sink to the bottom and stay there during the warmest months. Thus, the peaks of production generally occur in the early spring and in the autumn, when winds stir up the unstratified waters and allow nutrients to circulate freely to the well-lit upper layer where food generating takes place. Stratification also affects the distribution of dissolved oxygen; near the surface, oxygen is abundant as a result of diffusion from the atmosphere or algal photosynthesis, but it often becomes scarce at the bottom because of the decomposition of organic matter. Besides affecting the amount of algae that grows, thermal stratification helps determine the order in which different kinds of plant organisms bloom. In some lakes the waters are structured by a different kind of stratification, caused by chemical differences in density: Relatively pure water rides atop a pocket of dense water rich in dissolved salts. For example, Soap

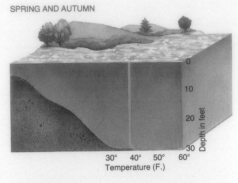

SPRING AND AUTUMN

MIDSUMMER

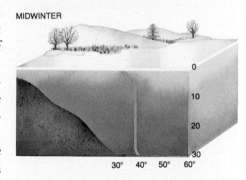

MIDWINTER

These diagrams show seasonal changes in the temperature layers of a typical temperate-zone lake. In spring and autumn *(top),* temperature is nearly uniform at all levels, as the colored bar indicates. In summer *(middle),* the sun-warmed water in the lake's top layer (epilimnion) is significantly less dense than the cold water in the bottom layer (hypolimnion), and the two, separated by the intermediate layer (metalimnion), resist mixing. In winter *(bottom),* when ice coats the lake surface, the warmest water is in the bottom layer.

Lake in the state of Washington is so transparent that during the summertime a great amount of solar heat reaches to the heavy, salt-rich lower layer, where it accumulates and lingers through the winter. Though the surface in winter may be covered with ice, the lower levels of water are almost hot enough to poach an egg.

From the broad foundation of phytoplankton, the food chain builds upward in a pyramid. The second level of this pyramid is dominated by the tiny animals that graze upon the algal "grass" — the zooplankton.

In fresh-water lakes, zooplankton consist mainly of three groups: rotifers, copepods and the crustaceans called water fleas. Water fleas such as Daphnia and some copepods are strong swimmers. They move vertically in response to light, swimming upward as darkness approaches and downward at dawn.

The zooplankton population, with its close link to the seasonal cycle of algal food supply, reaches its peak in the spring, shortly after phytoplankton bloom in abundance. In turn the zooplankton provide sustenance for the third major level of the lake food chain: the nektonic community, at the apex of the pyramid. *Nekton* — from the Greek for "swimming" — refers to all the large active swimmers able to move under their own power from one part of the lake to another. The most common representatives of this group are fish.

Many species of fish dine not only on zooplankton but on a smorgasbord of foods. Large predator fish consume small members of their own nektonic community. Other fish feed on plants rooted to the bottom along the lakeshore or on algae, or directly on the drifting phytoplankton. Yet another major source of sustenance is the insect larvae and other small invertebrates of the bottom-dwelling, or benthic, community. The typical lake bottom is home to insect larvae, snails, small crustaceans and flatworms, and in the sediments beneath lurk nematode worms, bristle worms and microscopic invertebrates.

Like their brethren on river bottoms, most of these benthic organisms subsist on particles of organic matter and associated fungi and bacteria. These particles come from decomposing aquatic rooted plants, from leaves and other material of terrestrial origin, or from decaying phytoplankton that descend from the food-generating upper layer of the lake. By converting these leftovers into body tissue that is then consumed by carnivores, these benthic animals contribute substantially to the lake's food chain.

Even fish such as smelt and some species of alewives and minnows, which are chiefly consumers of zooplankton, sometimes eat insect larvae and other benthic creatures. These fish visually select each copepod or other zooplankton that they swallow. They also accidentally capture other prey as

These photographs show the three main links in the food chain of a temperate-zone lake. In the picture at bottom left are minute plants, known as phytoplankton, and tiny animals — zooplankton — that consume them. Both of these life-forms provide food for the nektonic (actively swimming) community, which includes such creatures as the limpet *(middle)* and a fresh-water jellyfish *(right)*.

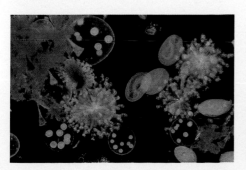

the water they ingest passes through their closely spaced gill rakers.

Larger fish such as trout and yellow perch are opportunistic feeders, dining on whatever is seasonally abundant. Perch, for example, may feed on zooplankton and even small fry of their own species during summer and early autumn; then they rely on benthic animals in winter and early spring. In Indiana's Wyland Lake, a biologist found that in July bluegill sunfish ate mostly water fleas. Then, as the water flea population declined, the sunfish shifted their attention to midge larvae on the lake bottom.

The wide variety of food available in many lakes makes it possible for even similar species of fish to coexist without competition. An unusual close-up of such peaceful coexistence was provided by the research of Peter B. Moyle. A graduate student at the University of Minnesota in 1966, Moyle set out that summer to study the feeding habits of fish in 164-acre Long Lake in Minnesota. The lake was known to contain 28 species of fish, including rainbow trout, bluegill sunfish, yellow perch, two kinds of darter and various types of minnow.

Moyle's work focused on three species of minnows, the most abundant fish in Long Lake. The three species appeared to be very similar: schools of all three species were often seen near one another in shallow water; they were believed to eat many of the same kinds of food and thus to be in competition. Here was an opportunity to study what ecologists call the competitive exclusion principle, which holds that complete competitors cannot coexist.

In order to learn more about what the minnows ate, Moyle collected weekly samples with a seine, netting fish both day and night and at different hours. He then examined and identified what was in their digestive tracts, a standard technique of research. Moyle also used another method, made possible here by the lake's exceptionally clear water. Using scuba gear, he swam underwater and was able to observe fish as well as plants and other bottom features. Surprisingly, as Moyle wrote later, "fishes were little disturbed by this procedure, even in shallow water." What Moyle observed in these underwater excursions, taken together with his analysis of gut contents, added up to a fascinating picture of specialization in feeding and other behavior by closely related species.

Moyle found that in the early morning one species, the mimic shiner, fed heavily on water fleas in the lake's middle depths. As the day advanced, the shiners fed near the surface or the bottom. They ceased feeding altogether after dark. Schools of mimic shiners, up to 15,000 strong, swam back and forth along the lakeshore as they fed. Toward evening, large schools broke into smaller groups, which swam to deeper water. At night, Moyle found the shiners lying inactive on the bottom.

The second species, blunt-nose minnows, also rested quietly on the bottom at night. By day they usually stayed in small schools near the bottom among plants, eating mostly insects, algae and detritus. Moyle found that members of the third minnow species, the common shiner, were roving opportunists. Regardless of the time of day, they fed wherever food was plentiful—on the bottom, among plants, in midwater or at the surface. In one sample, the shiner's guts were filled with midges that had been hatching at the surface. Another sample revealed that the shiners had fed largely on filamentous algae, found attached to solid surfaces in the lake bottom, including sticks and other flotsam.

Flowers Abloom in Crystal-Clear Ponds

A diver strains against the current of one of the races, or connecting waterways, that flow between the three Ewens Ponds in southern Australia. The crystal-clear ponds, copiously fed through fissures in a subterranean aquifer, discharge 36,000 gallons per minute into the race; this torrent thrusts aside stalks of Lilaeopsis, a plant that is related to celery.

Statistically, there is nothing impressive about the three Ewens Ponds, located a few miles inland from the south coast of Australia midway between Adelaide and Melbourne. The ponds are examples of a common type of lake, the sinkhole, that exists in large numbers throughout the world; they fill basins carved out by underground water, which dissolves cavities in limestone beds and causes the terrain above to collapse.

The three ponds are small and shallow (the largest is 100 feet across and 33 feet deep) and are linked by a narrow stream that empties into the Indian Ocean. By way of comparison, the nearby Piccaninnie Ponds *(overleaf)* are 188 feet deep at their deepest part, a drowned cavern so spacious that it is called the Cathedral.

The Ewens Ponds share one feature that makes them spectacular: water so incredibly clear that skin divers compare swimming in it to flying or walking in space. The ponds owe their clarity to several factors. Miles of limestone filter the water as it rises from deep aquifers. The tremendous influx of water — about 52 million gallons a day — keeps flushing out debris at an extraordinary rate. Moreover, the high level of dissolved

calcium in the water tends to precipitate silt and organic materials to the bottom. In all but the ponds' deepest parts, a great deal of sunlight reaches the bottom and fosters a lush growth of aquatic plants and flowers, which hold the silty debris in place.

These conditions have created an odd combination of riches and shortages. The ponds contain a fair number and variety of aquatic animals, among them species of snail, crustacean, turtle and trout. But with so much sunlight striking the bottom, the bouquets of water buttercup and the thickets of Triglochin photosynthesize with extraordinary vigor, saturating the waters with enough oxygen to support many additional aquatic creatures. Animal life is limited because the waters are low in the phosphorus and nitrogen needed to support phytoplankton, the basis of the food chain. The net result is that the ponds, which would age more rapidly if they had larger populations, retain both their crystalline clarity and their youth.

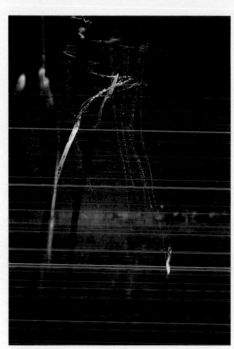

When they are punctured by nibbling snails, the leaves of underwater plants in Ewens Ponds release oxygen in streams that bubble visibly to the surface. More frequently, the oxygen that is released by aquatic plants is dissolved invisibly into the water instead.

A fresh-water crayfish, a lobster-like crustacean, inhabits Ewens Ponds. The crayfish is covered with parasites that feed on algae growing on its claws and shell.

◀ So clear is the water in the sinkholes of this region that divers, here in Piccaninnie Ponds, appear to be suspended in midair. Algae flourish only near the surface, creating a cascading garden in the shallows area. To avoid becoming disoriented in deeper water, the divers must be careful not to kick up silt and debris that have settled to the bottom.

Suspended in the sun-drenched water of Ewens Ponds, clusters of water buttercup mass around the ribbed stalks of Triglochin. The buttercups are able to protect themselves from this intense sunlight by adjusting the amount of red pigment in their leaves.

Moyle's unusual research over a two-year period thus showed that these three nearly identical species need not compete. Evolution had equipped Long Lake's minnows with adaptations in behavior that enabled them to occupy distinctly different ecological niches in the community.

The nektonic community in many lakes has higher life-forms than fish. The skillful, graceful otters are the fresh-water animals at the apex of the food chain in temperate climates; they consume fish, shellfish and, on occasion, water birds, muskrats and young beavers. In tropical Africa and South America, crocodiles or their close relatives dominate the top of the food chain, eating fish, birds and small or medium-sized animals, including an occasional human being.

All the creatures in a lake are influenced by the lake's natural aging process, which limnologists call eutrophication. Paradoxically, eutrophication steadily enriches a lake—and eventually causes its death. There are three stages in this process: oligotrophy—literally, little nourishment; mesotrophy—moderate nourishment; and eutrophy—abundant nourishment.

In its youth, the typical lake in a temperate region is oligotrophic. The water is clear, rich in dissolved oxygen at all levels but poor in essential plant nutrients such as nitrogen and phosphorus. This relative lack of fertility limits the production of phytoplankton and other plant life and thus restricts the profusion of animal life.

In middle age, the lake becomes mesotrophic. Nutrients flowing into the lake accumulate in the bottom sediments along with nutrients that have settled there from the decay of some of the lake's own organisms. Some of this nourishment may be recycled into the upper waters where it is photosynthesized into greater production of phytoplankton, which in turn supports larger populations of aquatic animals.

In the lake's old age, its fertility accelerates. Ever-increasing supplies of nutrients generate lush growth among rooted plants near the shore and among floating phytoplankton. Production of algae becomes dominated by mats of blue-green species that cover the surface like pea soup. The waters of the eutrophic lake are turbid with decaying organic matter from the increased populations of both plants and animals. This wholesale decomposition depletes the supply of dissolved oxygen in the lower levels of the lake—especially in deep lakes, where thermal stratification during the summer prevents the mixing of surface waters with bottom waters. In the absence of oxygen at the bottom, anaerobic bacteria attack the organic matter. This process releases hydrogen sulfide, a gas that smells like rotten eggs.

Though the stepped-up plant growth brings on a general increase in biological productivity, it also results in marked changes in the kinds of animals that inhabit the lake. For example, bottom-dwelling mayfly larvae and nymphs are replaced by midges, which need less oxygen. And all that organic matter piling up on the bottom, combined with sediments of silt and sand flowing in from tributaries, makes the lake shallower and thus warmer—with important consequences for the nektonic community. Fish life changes from forms that prefer deep, cold water to those that thrive in a warm, shallow environment. Trout and whitefish, for example, give way to bass and sunfish.

The filling in of a lake through eutrophication is inexorable but excruci-

Germany's Lake Charlotte, in its mesotrophic

middle age, contains a moderate amount of decayed organic matter and sustains a variety of flora and fauna.

atingly slow. Sediments may build up at an annual rate of only a tiny fraction of an inch; some English lakes took 8,000 years to accumulate 15 feet of organic sediment, and that rate is considered rapid. But as depth decreases, more and more plants take root on the shallow bottom and their remains, together with those of other organisms, eventually fill up the basin. The lake turns into a marsh. Terrestrial vegetation invades the area, and even the marsh disappears eventually.

Naturally lakes age at different rates. The deepest lakes and lakes with rocky, nutrient-poor watersheds remain youthfully oligotrophic after millions of years. Naturally, too, the rates of eutrophication differ regionally. In tropical Africa, for instance, lakes eutrophy more rapidly than in the temperate zone because the heat and humidity accelerate the growth and the decay of plants.

The normal process of eutrophication can be greatly accelerated by extraordinary changes in the environment. Just such a change prematurely aged an English lake called Hickling Broad. For centuries the lake had served as a roost for black-headed gulls that annually flew in from their breeding grounds to feed nearby. Then, during the short span of two decades, the gull population increased tenfold. The number of offshore fishing boats meanwhile declined, and with it the amount of waste offal thrown overboard; at the same time, the land-based food supply increased with the conversion of land to agriculture and the dumping of edible wastes on town rubbish heaps. With so many more gulls in the area, a great deal more of their phosphate-rich excrement wound up in Hickling Broad, overnourishing the algae and probably subtracting centuries from the lake's life span.

Often human beings hasten eutrophication more directly by what limnologists call cultural eutrophication. The most conspicuous causes are increased outpourings of sewage, industrial wastes and runoff from fertilized farms and barnyards — all of which contain nutrients that bring on premature aging in both lakes and rivers. In the Far East, where farmers often grow fish in ponds, cultural eutrophication is actually encouraged because it produces valuable protein for human consumption. Elsewhere, however, lakes are prized mainly as sources of drinking water and of recreation, and here cultural eutrophication is a serious problem, threatening even the largest lakes.

Scientific study of the record laid down by old sediments shows that cultural eutrophication is not a new problem. Paleolimnologists who examined the sediments at the bottom of Italy's Lago di Monterosi, a little lake north of Rome, found that the strata of plant and animal fossils embedded there told an extraordinary story of lake evolution and human change. From what the bottommost sediments revealed, the lake was youthfully oligotrophic and thus relatively unproductive for the first 24,000 years of its life. Then, about 2,100 years ago, a sudden change occurred. Blue-green algae proliferated, and sedimentation of both organic and inorganic matter began piling up rapidly.

These symptoms of sudden eutrophication recorded in the sediments coincided almost precisely with an event described in written history. About 171 B.C., the Romans began building a highway, the Via Cassia, that passed near the lake. During construction, crews of laborers cut down adjoining forests. This disrupted the drainage pattern of the area, trigger-

A moss-covered eutrophic lake in northwestern Canada reaches the end of its life cycle. Just before a lake dies, its plentiful nutrients promote dense populations of plants and animals. The lake grows shallower, and its oxygen is depleted as decaying organic matter clouds the water and builds up on the bottom. Eventually the lake will be completely filled in.

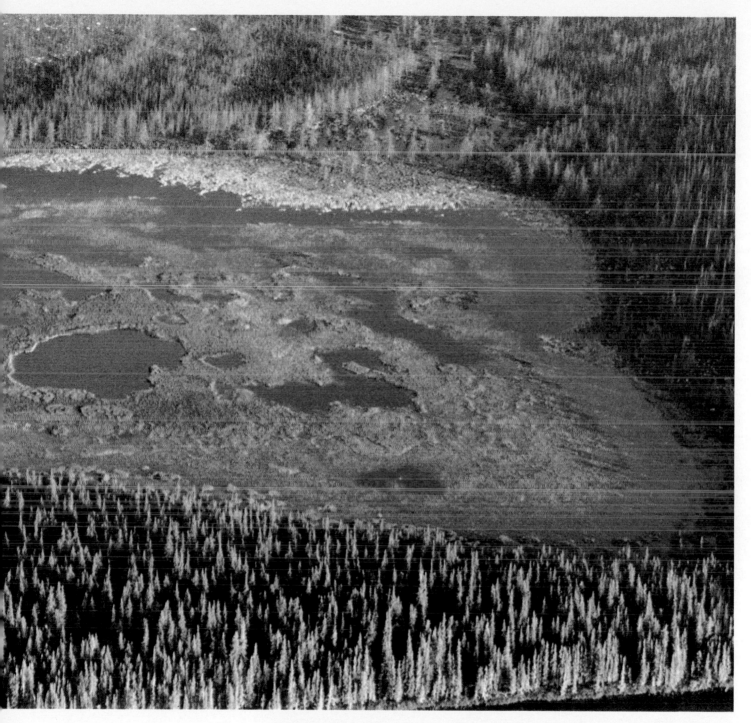

ing heavy runoff of nutrient-filled soil that the tree roots had helped keep in place. The result was a sudden burst of eutrophication and a rapid build-up of sedimentation.

A different kind of aging affects bodies of water classified as salt lakes. Every lake contains some dissolved minerals, but when the concentration of solutes exceeds 3 per cent by weight, it becomes a salt lake. (By comparison, the earth's oceans have an average salinity of 3.5 per cent.)

Saline lakes are surprisingly common, occupying nearly as much of the earth's surface as do fresh-water lakes. Salt lakes occur in arid regions of

Lake Moondarra in Australia, pictured at top in 1978, lies choked with about 50,000 metric tons of the fast-growing floating fern *Salvinia molesta*. Thus began an insect success story. Australian scientists learned that the *Cyrtobagous singularis* beetle, vignetted at center, serves as a natural herbicidal agent in the fern's native Brazil, and in 1980 they imported these beetles in an attempt to wipe out the blighting plant. By 1981, the fern-loving beetles had saved Lake Moondarra, achieving the cleanup seen in the picture at bottom.

every continent, including Antarctica; here the remarkable Lake Vanda is permanently covered with about 13 feet of ice, yet solar radiation and heat conduction from the lake bed maintain a temperature of 78° F. in the salty waters at its bottom. Saline lakes range in size from small seasonal ponds to the Caspian Sea, which has a surface area of 262,000 square miles.

The Caspian Sea is exceptional among salt lakes for its origin as well as for its size. Until about 290 million years ago, when tectonic uplift of the earth's crust made the Caspian an inland lake, it was part of the Mediterranean Sea. But since then, the influx from the Volga River and lesser streams — about 175 cubic miles of fresh water annually — has diluted the Caspian to an average salinity of only 1.27 per cent. Actually only certain parts of the Caspian now belong in the category of saline lakes.

Most salt lakes are quite the opposite of the Caspian Sea in that they started out as bodies of fresh water and got progressively saltier. Some become saline because their inflowing streams carry unusually high concentrations of minerals. More often, the cause is a geological paroxysm such as tectonic uplift that cuts off the lake's channel of outflow and thereby stops the flushing out of salts. In such a case, the lake's water evaporates faster than it can be replenished by inflow. Only the water evaporates; the minerals content is left in the lake, increasing the concentration of solutes. If evaporation continues to exceed outflow, the lake dries up and dies.

Such is the fate of the enormous ancient lake that geologists named Bonneville, which once covered 20,000 square miles in the American West. Meltwater from the most recent ice age filled Bonneville's basin about 13,000 years ago. Then, with inflow less than outflow and evaporation, it dried up, leaving as a remnant Utah's Great Salt Lake, which is North America's biggest and saltiest body of inland water, with a salinity averaging 22 per cent. Though a recent succession of wet winters has reversed the general trend, the lake is expected to resume its long-term shrinkage; in the past century or so its area has dwindled from 2,400 to 1,600 square miles.

Great Salt Lake is exceeded in salinity only by the historic body of water that occupies a deep trench in the earth's crust between Israel and Jordan: the Dead Sea. Salinity there averages 28 per cent. When fish wash in from the Jordan River or one of the other tributaries, they die almost instantly. Only the most halophilic, or salt-loving, organisms can survive: one species of green algae and several species of microorganisms. One of the bacteria provides a purple pigment that is among the few known biological substances capable of converting sunlight directly into energy through photosynthesis.

The killing salinity of the Dead Sea has led to a popular belief that salt lakes are biological deserts. The truth is that many of these mineral-rich lakes are extraordinarily productive. They contain a variety of organisms, which range from phytoplankton and zooplankton through insect larvae and crustaceans and even include fish. Typically, the fish are freshwater species that have developed a high tolerance for lake salts, rather than species of marine origin.

One of the bleakest but most productive saline lakes is Southern California's Salton Sea. This large body of salty water was formed by a flood in 1905, when the Colorado River overflowed the entrance to a canal that had been constructed to bring water for irrigation to the lower end of the California desert. The Salton Sea has a salinity approaching 6 per cent and is surrounded by hills so desolate that the area was once used for the filming of Dante's *Inferno*. Nonetheless, the lake supports a lively sports fishery of salt-tolerant corvina that reach lengths of two and a half feet.

A striking adaptation to salinity has taken place in the salt lakes of East Africa, which support half of the earth's population of flamingos. These stunning, long-legged birds with pink plumage depend upon the lakes' blue-green algae and zooplankton for food and upon dry portions of the lake bed for breeding. The salt crust and the heat prevent animal predators from crossing the lakes to reach the flamingos' mud nests.

Many limnologists study salt lakes in preference to fresh-water ones, for the ecosystems of such lakes have fewer variables, making it easier to isolate and solve difficult basic problems. In fact, one of the most thoroughly investigated biotas is that of Mono, a salt lake in eastern California that Mark Twain once described as "solemn, silent, sailless . . . the lovely tenant of the loneliest spot on Earth." Nestling in the arid eastern shadow of the 13,000-foot-high Sierra Nevada, Mono is one of the oldest continuously existing lakes on the North American continent, having occupied part of a 25-mile-wide basin for a period of at least 730,000 years and probably longer. Though melting Sierran glaciers caused the lake to overflow briefly during the last ice age, no river, ancient or modern, has ever drained it. All of its inflow eventually evaporates, leaving ever-higher concentrations of minerals.

Mono's resulting chemistry makes its waters both salty and bitter to the taste. Its salinity, which is nearly three times that of the Atlantic, derives mostly from sodium chloride—ordinary table salt. The bitter taste comes from carbonates, principally sodium carbonate, which is a relative of baking soda. Because of these high carbonate concentrations the water is 80 times as alkaline as sea water. "Its sluggish waters are so strong with alkali," wrote Mark Twain, "that if you only dip the most hopelessly soiled garment into them once or twice, and wring it out, it will be found as clean as if it had been through the ablest of washerwoman's hands."

The carbonates also give rise to tall deposits of a mineral called tufa. Like the stalactites and stalagmites that festoon caves, tufa is composed of calcium carbonate, which is the principal mineral in limestone. The tufa structures are built up around the mouths of fresh-water springs at the bottom of a lake as calcium bubbles up and combines chemically with the lake's carbonates. As the lake water receded over the millennia, many of the old tufa towers were exposed, becoming landmarks on the shore. Springs still flow from some of them.

Mono's bizarre chemistry supports only a few life-forms, but those species multiply and grow at astonishing rates. Phosphates and other minerals furnish the nutrients, and every spring the desert sun cooks a rich soup of several species of blue-green algae. Most of the algae is consumed by two types of animals, tiny brine shrimp and the young of the brine fly Hydropyrus. With no other animals competing for food, the shrimp and the flies proliferate to astronomical numbers. As many as 4,000 flies have been counted in a single square foot of shore. "Their buzz," wrote a 19th Century journalist, was "like the brewing of a distant storm."

The brine fly gave Mono Lake its name. In the language of the Yokut Indians, who lived in the Yosemite region west of the lake, *mono* meant "brine fly." It also meant "fly people," and the Yokut used the word to refer to the Paiute Indians, who lived near the lake's foam-covered shore and there gathered as food the brine fly's larvae and pupae. The Paiute fly harvest took place at the end of each summer. "They come from far and near to gather them," wrote William Brewer in 1863. "The worms [pupae] are dried in the sun, the shell rubbed off, when a yellowish kernel remains, like a small grain of rice. This is oily, very nutritious, and not unpleasant to the taste. The Indians gave me some. It does not taste bad, and if one were ignorant of its origins, it would make a fine soup."

Mono's brine shrimp are a species, *Artemia monica,* that cannot survive in any other saline habitats. (On the other hand, brine shrimp from Great Salt Lake, which is more than twice as salty, die when placed in Mono Lake.) Only three eighths of an inch long, Mono's shrimp are fringed with 11 pairs of feathery appendages that gracefully propel them as they graze upon the algae. The shrimp are so light that it takes about 6,000 to make a pound. Approximately 250 tons of them are harvested each year for sale as food for hatchery trout and for tropical fish in aquariums. This is only a tiny fraction of the available supply. At times of peak density, 50,000 shrimp crowd into a single cubic yard of lake water, and there may be as many as four trillion in the entire lake.

No fish dine upon Mono's abundance of shrimp and flies. When the California authorities attempted to stock the lake with trout nearly a half century ago, the fish "made three jumps," an official noted, "and then turned belly up." Clearly the lake's water was too salty to sustain trout.

The absence of fish — and hence of competition for food — attracts hordes of water birds to Mono to feed upon the virtually inexhaustible supply of shrimp and flies. No fewer than 79 species — nearly every kind of North American shore bird, duck grebe and gull — visit Mono. On a single day, about 800,000 birds have been seen feeding there.

The lake is the breeding ground for as many as 50,000 California gulls, 95 per cent of the state's population. In the fall, an estimated 700,000 eared grebes — perhaps 80 per cent of the earth's population — drop in at Mono on their way south. Mono is also a late-summer refueling stop for 100,000 Wilson's phalaropes on their 5,000-mile journey from nesting grounds in southern Canada to their winter homes in South America. Feasting on flies and shrimp, these little creatures nearly double their weight during their stopover at Mono, storing up energy for the long flight south.

Limnologists have studied Mono's ecosystem in such detail in recent years because they fear that the lake is literally being drained of life. Of course Mono has always lost prodigious amounts of water to evaporation by the hot desert sun. But for many decades the annual loss of 40 inches was just about balanced by the inflow from springs and from the five fresh-water tributary streams, and the lake's level remained roughly constant.

Then, in 1941, the city of Los Angeles began tapping Mono's lifeblood. To satisfy the needs of that city, water was diverted from the lake's tributary streams and sent 275 miles south through an elaborate aqueduct system. A second aqueduct was completed in 1958, which doubled the diversion of water. Today all but one of Mono's five tributaries have been tapped, and diversions take 60 per cent of all the water that would ordinarily flow into the lake.

The effect on the lake was summed up a few years ago by Wallis McPher-

Columns of tufa (calcium carbonate) loom above California's Mono Lake like the towers and bastions of a fantastic castle. These mineral structures were built by subterranean springs, whose calcium-bearing waters interact with the calcium carbonate and other chemicals concentrated in the salt lake.

son, a lifelong resident of the Mono area. The lake, he said, "went down to hell and gone." Since diversions began, the water level has dropped 45 feet. The lake's volume has been cut in half, nearly doubling its salinity to 9.5 per cent. Its surface area, once 86 square miles, has been reduced by nearly 30 per cent. More than 25 square miles of salt-encrusted bottom have been exposed to windstorms that stir dense clouds of alkaline dust thousands of feet into the air.

In the late 1970s, reports of Mono's slow demise brought many limnologists there to study the biological effects of its shrinkage and its increasing salinity. One dramatic consequence became evident almost immediately. Toward the end of 1978 the falling water level exposed enough bottom to serve as a land bridge to Negit Island, a nesting site for as many as 30,000 California gulls. The island previously had provided sanctuary for the birds' eggs and newly hatched chicks, but now the way was open for coyotes and other predators from the mainland.

California National Guardsmen attempted to reopen the channel of water and restore Negit Island's isolation. Twice during the spring of 1979 they tried unsuccessfully to blast the land bridge out of existence with explosives. That summer, coyotes invaded the island in force and, recalls one researcher, "Not a chick survived."

In 1980 the state of California managed to keep the coyotes out by erecting a chain-link fence, topped with barbed wire, across the two-mile breadth of the land bridge. But the gulls, after their disastrous experience the previous year, refused to return to Negit Island. In decreased numbers, they crowded onto smaller islands in Mono Lake. If the waters continue to recede, these islands too will soon become connected to the mainland and thus be lost as nesting sanctuaries.

Researchers foresee other dire consequences as well. If diversion of inflow

A Wilson's phalarope, foraging along the shore of Mono Lake, fattens for its winter migration by gorging on the brine flies and brine shrimp that swarm around the algae-rich lake. During a late-summer sojourn at Mono, the phalarope may double its weight.

Reddish brine shrimp flourish in the waters of Mono Lake, feasting on the abundant summertime crop of algae. Between the death of one shrimp generation in the autumn and the hatching of the next in the spring, rampant algae growth turns the lake a soupy green.

continues at the present rate, salinity will reach 20 per cent soon after the turn of the century. In water that salty, experiments already have demonstrated, Mono's unique shrimp will die and brine-fly larvae probably will not survive. The death of these creatures would mean the loss of a vital refueling stop for migratory birds and, indeed, of a unique natural laboratory for ecological research.

Hoping to save the lake, environmental groups launched lawsuits against Los Angeles and pressed for legislation that would force the city to curtail its diversions by 85 per cent. Los Angeles officials opposed any change, citing their city's dependence on the water. The diversions not only account for 17 per cent of the city's water supply but also — by passing through electrical turbines en route to Los Angeles — generate 2 per cent of its power supply.

In any case, city officials say, Mono will not be drained — as so many other lakes in the American West have been — to supply cities and irrigate farms; a different but nonetheless gloomy fate awaits the lake. The officials' projections indicate that Mono will stop shrinking toward the middle of the next century, when decreasing evaporation from its vastly reduced surface will be offset by underground springs and by the trickle that gets through from its tributaries.

Then Mono will stabilize — about 50 feet below its present level and with a surface area one third of what it was before diversion began. At that point Mono's salinity will equal or exceed that of the Dead Sea, and Mono too will become an all-but-lifeless chemical sump. Although two wet winters in the early 1980s raised the lake's water level by nine feet, no permanent relief is expected from the weather. The only way to halt the decline of Mono Lake lies in proposed legislation to curtail the diversion of water from tributary streams. **Ω**

A HELLISH LAKE OF MUD AND SODA

Sprawling in the Rift Valley midway between two great African landmarks, Lake Victoria and the twin peaks of Kilimanjaro, Lake Natron is 500 square miles of hell: suffocating equatorial heat, bitter waters and vile-smelling mud encrusted with alkali. Midday temperatures as high as 150° F. evaporate the lake's water eight times as fast as the sparse rainfall can replenish it. But geysers keep feeding the lake a caustic brew of soda (sodium carbonate) from volcanically heated underground springs, and streams flowing over alkaline volcanic soil carry in still more soda.

In places, the soda build-up is thick enough and hard enough to walk on. But the crust of alkali is treacherous, as a British scientist discovered when he set out to explore the flats on foot. He broke through the alkali and floundered in the mud. Corrosive soda filled his boots and inflicted cruel burns and blisters. It took skin grafts to repair the damage.

Only one large animal is fully adapted to Natron's inhospitable environment: the flamingo. Two species of the spectacular bird, the greater flamingo and the lesser flamingo, inhabit this lake and several others in the Rift Valley; about three million of them, half the world's flamingo population, thrive on the tons of algae that tint the alkaline water green. The birds' diet is fortified with abundant insects, among them mole crickets, earwigs and dragonflies, and by small crustaceans such as brine shrimp. Except for these life-forms, Lake Natron is virtually sterile.

Reflecting a tranquil sky and clouds, Natron's mirror-smooth water is surrounded by grim flats of black mud and white soda. The reflection frequently disorients migrating birds; many of them, lured from normal flight, plunge into the lethally alkaline waters.

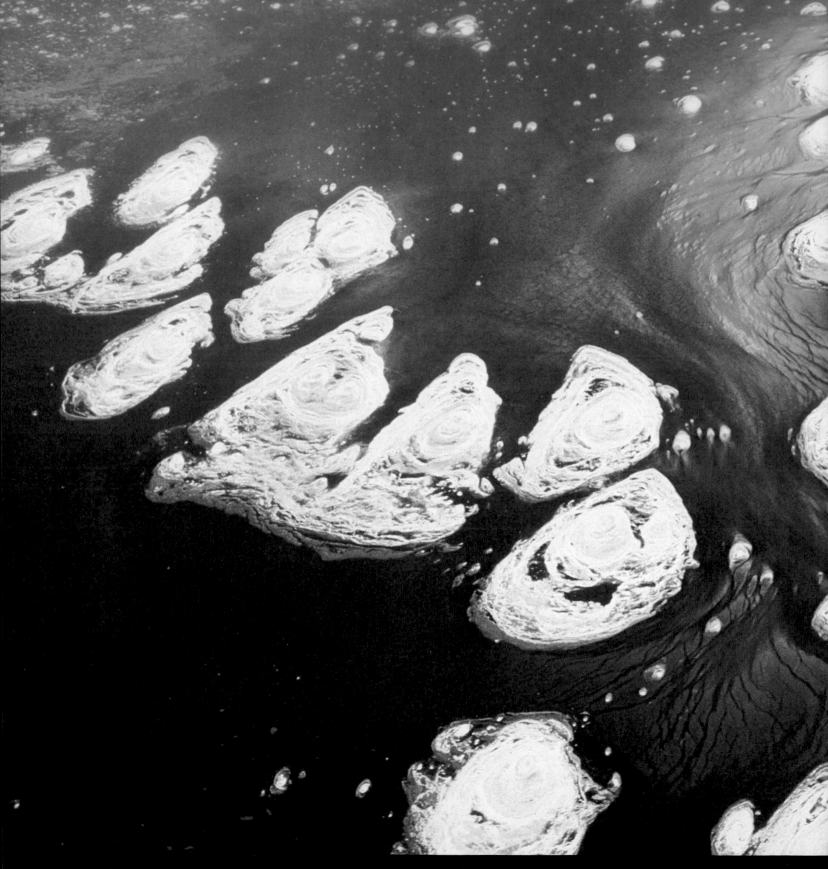

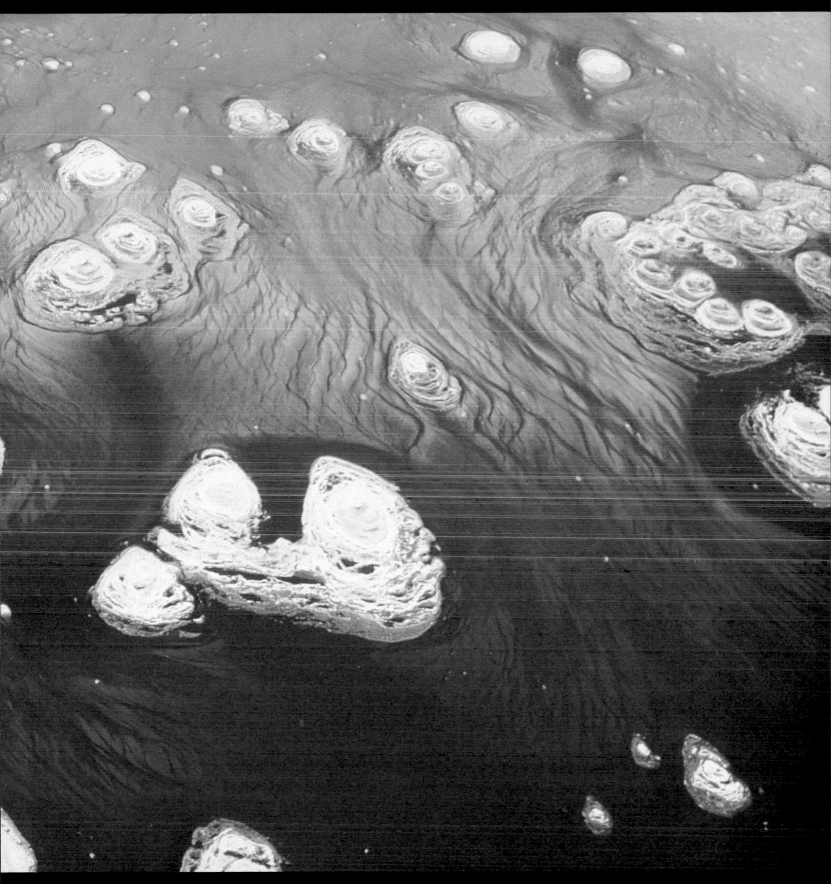

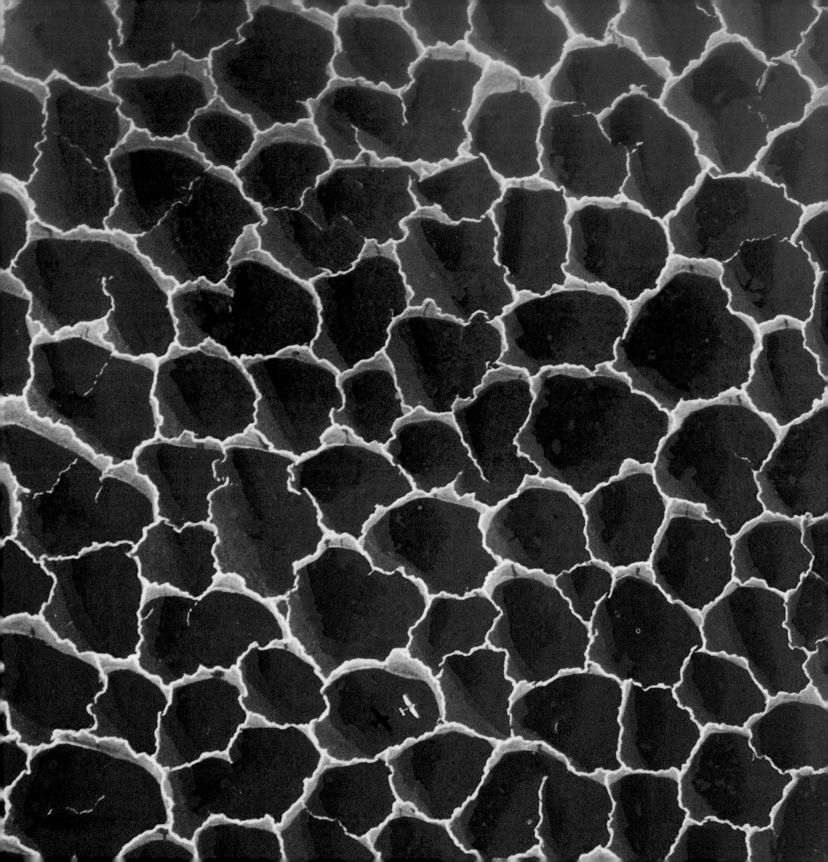

purple-red pigment is one of the very few known
biochemical substances besides chlorophyll
that can transform sunlight into food.

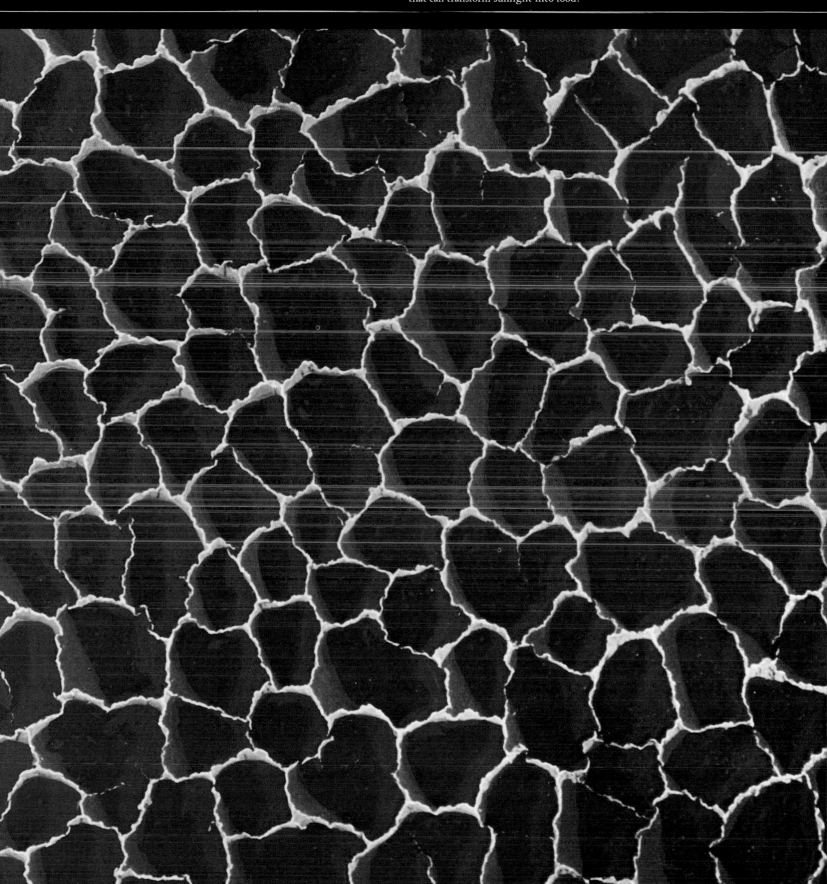

Floating sheets of soda, resembling ice floes adrift on a polar sea, encircle a pair of geysers on Lake Natron. Such floes, which form as evaporation increases the concentration of minerals in the lake, are kept afloat by gas bubbles that are inside the soda masses.

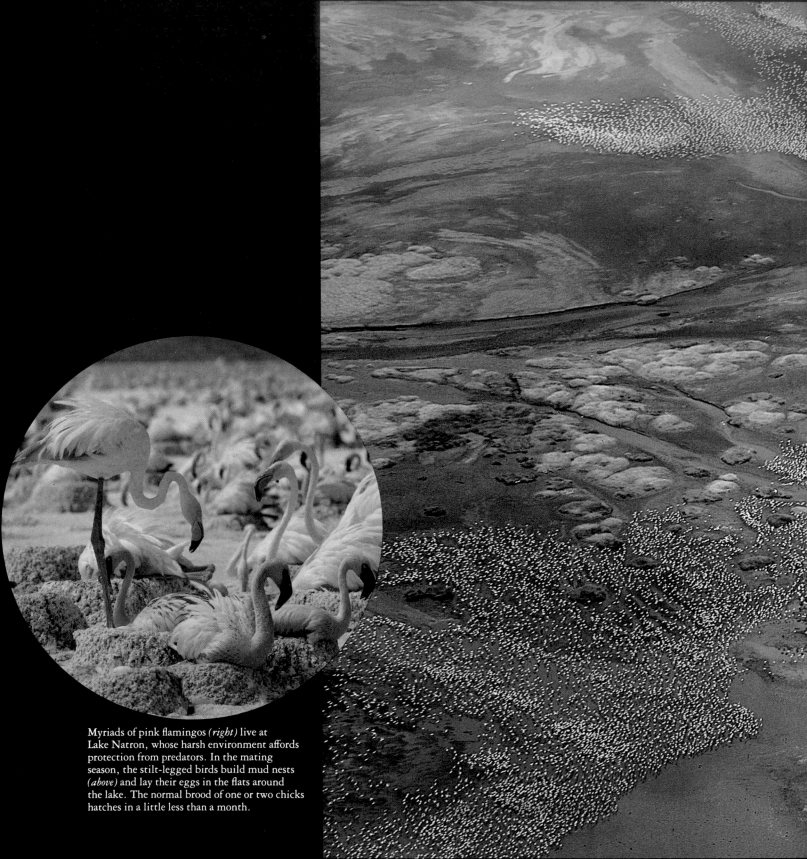

Myriads of pink flamingos *(right)* live at
Lake Natron, whose harsh environment affords
protection from predators. In the mating
season, the stilt-legged birds build mud nests
(above) and lay their eggs in the flats around
the lake. The normal brood of one or two chicks
hatches in a little less than a month.

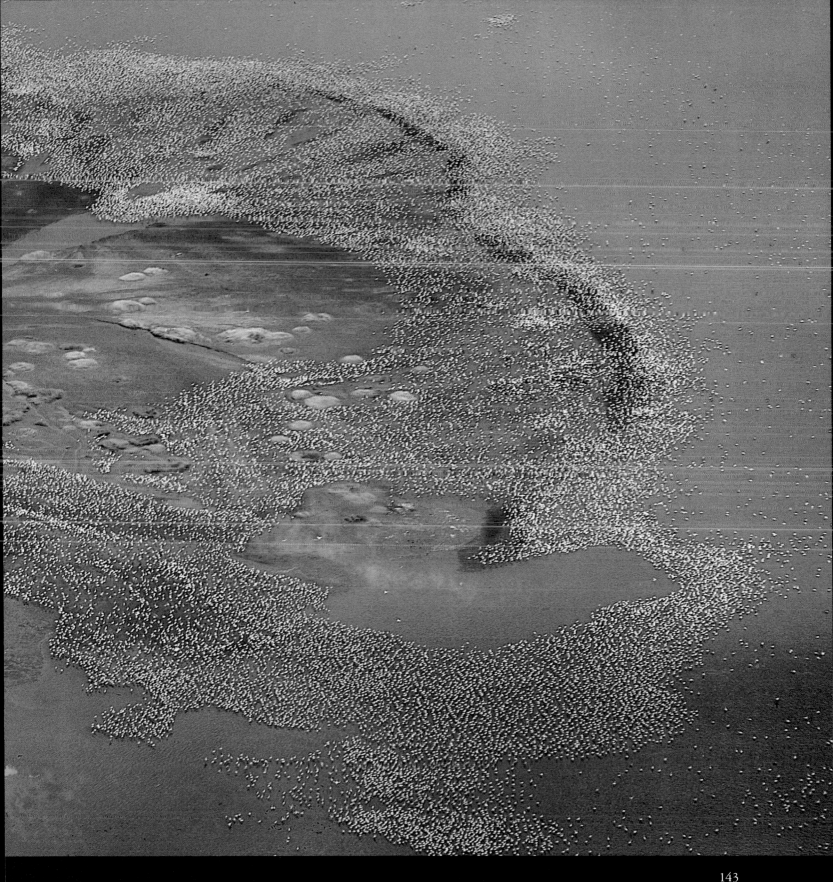

Chapter 5

THE FRESH-WATER OCEANS

The French Jesuit missionaries who came upon the Great Lakes in the 17th Century thought they were oceans. It was a natural mistake, for the five lakes do seem limitless in extent. Lake Superior's 31,800 square miles make it the world's largest fresh-water lake. (The Caspian Sea, originally an arm of the Mediterranean Sea, is larger and technically a lake because it is now landlocked, but it is a salt-water lake.) Huron, Michigan, Erie and even the smallest of the Great Lakes, Ontario, rank among the world's 15 largest fresh-water lakes.

The Great Lakes are more awesome still when they are viewed as an entity, linked to one another by rivers or straits. The five lakes form one continuous navigable waterway that stretches 2,342 miles from Duluth, Minnesota, at the western tip of Lake Superior, to the entrance of the St. Lawrence River, at Kingston, Ontario. The entire lake system covers nearly 95,000 square miles, an expanse larger than the United Kingdom. With the exception of Superior, which is as much as 1,300 feet deep, the lakes are relatively shallow. Yet they are so vast that their volumes total approximately 5,500 cubic miles of water — one fifth of the earth's standing fresh water.

In size and scientific interest, the Great Lakes are matched by only one other body of fresh water: Lake Baikal in eastern Siberia. Baikal has a surface area of 12,000 square miles, a size that makes the lake rank fifth among fresh-water lakes, but smaller than Superior, Huron or Michigan. What makes Baikal extraordinary is its depth. Filling a great chasm more than a mile deep, it contains approximately 5,500 cubic miles of water — equal to all the Great Lakes combined.

Thus Baikal and the Great Lakes together hold 40 per cent of the earth's liquid fresh water. This fact, along with their fascinating geological histories and their astonishing varieties of aquatic life, has made these greatest of the earth's lakes a subject of intense interest to scientists.

In 1979, a delegation of American scientists traveled to the Soviet Union to attend the first international symposium aimed at comparing Baikal and the Great Lakes. The scientists found obvious differences. The Great Lakes lie in a temperate climate at the center of the North American industrial heartland, which has a population of more than 37 million; Baikal lies in the remote, sub-Arctic wilderness of central Asia, more than 30 miles from the nearest city, Irkutsk. The Great Lakes are extremely young, only a few thousand years old; Baikal is probably the earth's oldest lake, dating back 25 million years. The American visitors were also struck by the similarities

Lapped by waves, a pebble-strewn beach on sea-like Lake Superior stretches off to the horizon — part of a shoreline more than three quarters the length of the U.S. Atlantic coast. Because Superior and a few other lakes are so vast, they are longer lived and slower to change than lakes of ordinary size.

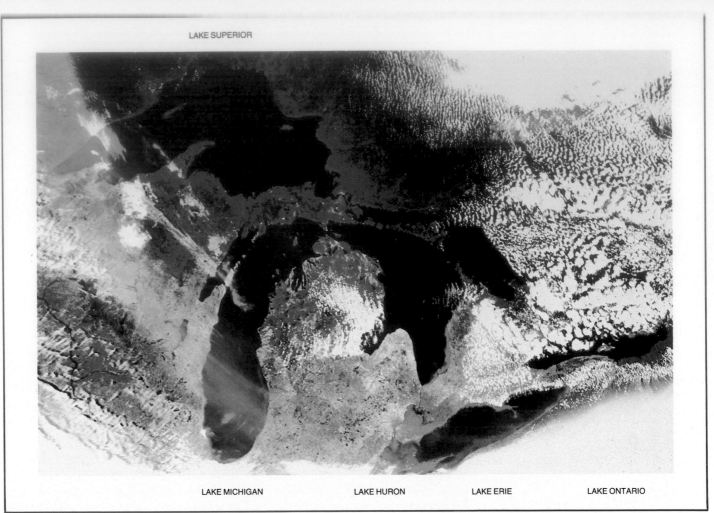

LAKE SUPERIOR

LAKE MICHIGAN LAKE HURON LAKE ERIE LAKE ONTARIO

between Baikal and Lake Superior. Both lakes are big, deep and cold; both lie in basins of dense, durable rock that yield only small amounts of soluble minerals; and the waters of both have a dazzling transparency.

The Great Lakes, shown here in a computerized satellite photograph, span a distance of 800 miles across central and east-central North America. The five lakes constitute a drainage basin for about one fiftieth of the continent.

By virtue of their central location, the Great Lakes came under scientific scrutiny long before Baikal. Though geologists had previously prospected along the shores for minerals, the first purely scientific expedition to the lakes was mounted during the summer of 1848 by Louis Agassiz. The famed Swiss naturalist had proposed that immense sheets of ice once covered parts of the earth. These glaciers — not a catastrophic flood, as many scientists previously believed — had carved out the basins of many lakes and shaped other natural features, sculpting the landscape, in Agassiz's felicitous phrase, like "God's great plough."

Agassiz, a professor of geology at Harvard, took nine students and six fellow scientists on a leisurely study of Lake Superior's northern shore. Accompanying the expedition were a dozen French Canadians and Ojibwa Indians, who served as guides. Agassiz led the way in a canoe with a large frying pan lashed to the prow as its figurehead.

Agassiz's two-month-long sojourn on Lake Superior produced important new evidence, in the form of boulders transported by glaciers from farther north, that glaciers had carved the basins of the five Great Lakes. But Agassiz also came to the conclusion — and modern investigators agree — that it would be "a great mistake to ascribe the present form of Lake Superior to any single geological event." In fact, the lakes were formed by a complex combination of events (*pages 150-151*) that radically revamped the drainage pattern of the North American interior.

146

As a result, Lake Superior and its more than 200 tributaries serve as the headwaters of the entire five-lake system. The water from the many short, swift-flowing streams that drain into Superior eventually passes through Lakes Huron, Erie and Ontario before exiting from the system through the St. Lawrence River and entering the Atlantic Ocean — a distance of nearly 1,600 miles.

The early stages of this journey are excruciatingly slow. Because the area drained by Superior is relatively small for a lake of its size and because the lake's volume is so great (2,900 cubic miles, or more than half of the Great Lakes' total), water remains within Superior for more than a century.

Very gradually, the water follows a descending series of geological stair-steps. From Superior's elevation of 600 feet above sea level, water flows down the St. Mary's River (and through the man-made canal and locks at Sault Ste. Marie) to Lake Huron. Huron also receives input from Lake Michigan, whose waters flow into Huron through the Straits of Mackinac. Both lakes lie 579 feet above sea level and behave as one body of water in matters of flow.

Water from these three upper lakes eventually flows out of Lake Huron into the St. Clair River, through shallow Lake St. Clair and down the Detroit River into Lake Erie. With a mean depth of just 58 feet, Erie is the shallowest of the Great Lakes.

Erie's water, 570 feet above sea level, flows north into the Niagara River, where it drops 225 feet within a distance of 35 miles; most of the descent occurs at Niagara Falls. The water, well oxygenated by its fall, flows via the lower Niagara River to Lake Ontario, the smallest but third deepest lake in the system, with a maximum depth of 802 feet and a mean depth of 283 feet. Ontario retains its inflow for about eight years. Its outflow pours into the St. Lawrence River at the prodigious volume of 233,000 cubic feet per second, then travels northeastward for about 750 miles to the Gulf of St. Lawrence and finally into the North Atlantic.

The water that follows this route derives in part from the rivers and streams that flow into the Great Lakes, the great majority of them emptying into Superior. These tributaries and the Great Lakes themselves drain an area of 194,000 square miles, a region about the size of Spain. However, this is a relatively small drainage area, representing only about twice the total surface area of the lakes; most big lakes drain regions at least six times as large as their own surfaces.

Because their drainage area is so small, the Great Lakes also depend heavily upon the inflow of groundwater and of rain and snow that fall directly on their surfaces to compensate for the loss of water through outflow and evaporation. The average annual precipitation on the lakes increases from west to east, ranging from 29 inches on Lake Superior to 34 inches on Erie and Ontario. An estimated one half of the lakes' volume comes directly from this precipitation.

As a consequence, extreme fluctuations in the amount of rain or snow can profoundly influence water levels. Prolonged drought lowers the level by as much as 10 feet, leaving boat moorings high and dry; excessive precipitation can raise the level by 10 feet and cause serious flooding along the shore.

The precipitation that falls on the lakes is relatively pristine, but once in their basins, it takes on a chemical complexity influenced by the geology of the region. Geologically, the lakes cut across the boundary between the

Swiss naturalist Louis Agassiz, shown at left illustrating a marine invertebrate, proposed the basic theory of ice-age glaciation in 1848, the year he led a scientific expedition to Lake Superior. Agassiz deduced correctly that the rocks along the shores of the lake *(below)* had been grooved and gouged as glaciers carved out the basins for the Great Lakes.

Precambrian Canadian Shield on the north, dating from nearly one billion years ago, and younger Paleozoic formations farther south. The Canadian Shield's ancient metamorphic and igneous rocks weather slowly, yielding few nutrients and leaving Superior and part of Huron profoundly oligotrophic — rich in oxygen and silica, poor in phosphorus, cold and clear. Sunlight penetrates to a depth of 125 feet in Lake Superior. Because of the lack of nutrients, the land around Superior and Huron is made up of thin, relatively infertile soil that is difficult to farm.

Lakes Michigan, Erie and Ontario rest on shales and other Paleozoic sediments, as well as on extensive glacial deposits up to 600 feet thick. The glacial deposits have clouded these lakes with leached nutrients and enriched the surrounding terrain, which yields plentiful crops of grains, fruits and other agricultural products.

All of the five Great Lakes benefit agriculture by moderating the climate; by absorbing and storing great quantities of heat, the lakes tend to produce cooler summers and milder winters. This absorption of heat also causes the growing season near the lakes to lag, delaying spring flowering in orchards and vineyards until after the last frost but holding off autumn frosts until crops mature.

The lakes exert a less benign influence on winter precipitation. Air moving from west to east takes on moisture and warmth from the water. When this warmer, moisture-laden air encounters the cold land mass at the eastern shores of the Great Lakes, intense blizzards often engulf the so-called snowbelt of upstate New York. Buffalo, on the eastern shore of Lake Erie, receives an average of 85 inches of snow a year.

Scientists studying the Great Lakes have long been fascinated by dramatic and dangerous fluctuations in the lakes' water levels. Such a sudden oscillation is known as a surge, or seiche, a word originally applied to a tidelike rise and fall in Switzerland's Lake Geneva.

Seiches are caused by atmospheric disturbances such as locally strong winds and variations in barometric pressure. Once begun, the oscillations continue even after the variations disappear. The result has been likened to water sloshing back and forth in a bathtub. In the case of the Great Lakes, however, the tub may be several hundred miles long, and the seiches may involve hundreds of cubic miles of water. The seiches that slosh back and forth across Lake Erie, for example, sometimes disrupt shipping timetables. Erie is so shallow that large freighters must carefully coordinate their entry into harbors with the high end of the seiche or risk running aground. The highest surge ever measured on the Great Lakes occurred on Lake Erie on January 2, 1942: At Buffalo, the lake stood 13½ feet higher than at Toledo, 250 miles to the west.

There have been other seiches that have brought tragedy to the lakes. On June 26, 1954, a fast-moving squall roared across Lake Michigan at 66 mph. The squall generated a 10-foot-high wall of water that crashed ashore near Chicago and drowned seven people.

Because of their location between contrasting polar and tropical air masses, the Great Lakes are notorious for their sudden storms; the vast size of the lakes often makes these tempests oceanic in scale. November, coming at the end of the shipping season, can be the cruelest month on the lakes. In one memorable year, 1913, the gales of November claimed 40 ships and 235 lives. A mid-November storm in 1975 caused one of the lakes' most

How the Great Lakes Were Formed

Scientists realized more than a century ago that glaciers played a major role in creating the Great Lakes. But only in the last few decades, with the development of sophisticated new research tools, have geologists been able to reconstruct in detail the evolution of the lakes and the surrounding terrain *(key, below)* during the closing stages of the last ice age.

In the 1960s, for example, researchers working near the small town of Two Creeks, Wisconsin, found remnants of an ancient forest whose trees had been buried by rocks and soil from an advancing glacier. Using radiocarbon analysis, the researchers learned that the forest had been felled 11,850 years ago. This added to their knowledge of short-term changes in the Ice Age climate.

According to the latest findings, the Great Lakes took about 13,500 years to evolve from a series of ancestral lakes. At the start of this period, glaciers covered the heartland of the continent with ice up to 11,500 feet thick; the ice's colossal weight depressed the terrain around the lakes by as much as 1,500 feet. In the course of their periodic advances, the glaciers hollowed out lake basins from what had been large stream valleys. During the intervals of glacial retreat, the ice sheet filled the basins with meltwater and left behind great arc-shaped ridges of rocky debris up to several miles long and 600 feet high. These moraines helped revamp the region's drainage pattern as the ice sheet retreated: They plugged up outlets to the south while new outlets opened to the east.

BARREN

TUNDRA AND TAIGA

BOREAL FOREST

MIXED HARDWOODS

DECIDUOUS FOREST

GLACIAL ICE

Early Lake Chicago

Lake Maumee

17,000 YEARS AGO: As the continental glacier retreats, the southernmost ancestral lakes — Early Lake Chicago and Lake Maumee — begin to form near their present-day successors, Lakes Michigan and Erie, indicated by dotted lines. Because the glacier prevents the ancient lakes from draining northward, the overflow of glacial meltwater cuts channels that drain southward into the Mississippi River.

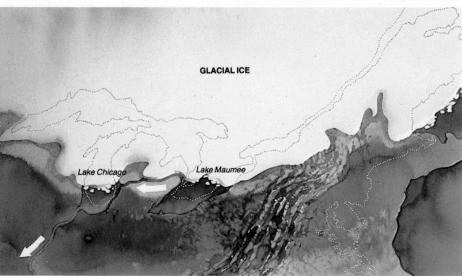

GLACIAL ICE

Lake Chicago

Lake Maumee

14,000 YEARS AGO: The continuing retreat of the ice sheet exposes a river that drains westward and downslope from Lake Maumee into Lake Chicago. This flow lowers Maumee's water level and stops the lake from draining southward through its earlier, higher outlet.

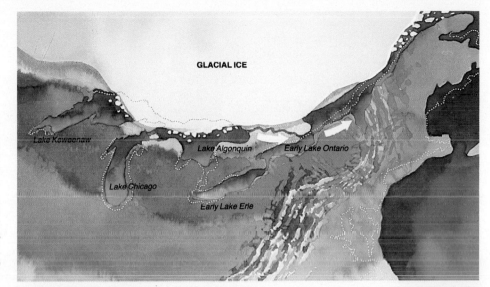

12,000 YEARS AGO: During the extended period of glacial retreat, meltwater from the ice sheet forms Lakes Keweenaw, Chicago, Algonquin, Early Erie and Early Ontario — the respective ancestors of modern Lakes Superior, Michigan, Huron, Erie and Ontario. Drainage along the future course of the St. Lawrence River also emerges, providing the lakes with a broad eastern outlet to the sea. As the lakes' water levels decline in response, the southern outlets for the western lakes run dry.

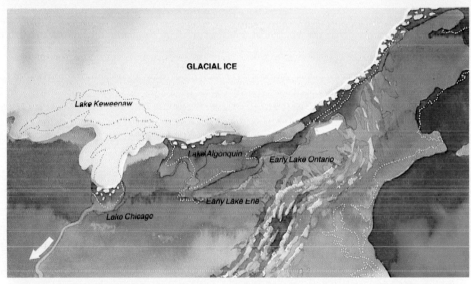

11,500 YEARS AGO: Another glacial advance across the depressed terrain surrounding the western lakes covers Lake Keweenaw completely and raises the water level of Lake Chicago enough to reopen its high southern outlet. In this period there are no major changes in the other lakes and their eastern outlets.

3,500 YEARS AGO: At this time the Great Lakes have almost achieved their present form and are draining eastward. The depressed terrain around the western lakes, rebounding in response to the final recession of the ice sheet, continues to rise after this period, until the lakes reach their present elevations.

storied tragedies, the loss of the 729-foot-long ore carrier *Edmund Fitzgerald*. Buffeted for hours by 30-foot waves and winds gusting to 70 knots near the eastern end of Lake Superior, the *Fitz* broke in half without warning and disappeared with all 29 crewmen in 530 feet of water.

The dangers inherent in the use of the Great Lakes cut both ways. Encroaching civilization has seriously damaged the fabric of life in the lakes, altering their entire ecosystem from the microscopic plankton at the bottom of the food chain to the predator fish at the top. One result has been a reduction in the bounty that the lakes provide.

From the beginning of the European invasion of the region, settlers thrived on the fish they found in the Great Lakes. The lakes abounded with succulent species such as lake trout, sturgeon, whitefish and lake herring. There were also plentiful yellow perch, deepwater sculpins and burbot. Probably the most prized catch for early anglers was the Atlantic salmon. This species existed only in Lake Ontario; here the world's largest known fresh-water population of Atlantic salmon was prevented from reaching Erie and the other Great Lakes by the precipitous barrier at Niagara Falls.

Lake Ontario's supply of Atlantic salmon dwindled rapidly during the 19th Century. The chief cause of the decline was not the fishermen's heavy catches but human tampering with the lakes' tributaries, where spawning took place and where young salmon normally spent their first two years of life. Dams were built for powering water mills, and they blocked the salmon's passage up many tributaries. Cultivated fields leached soil that silted up the salmon's gravelly spawning grounds.

Worst of all was the destruction of the dense forests that had shaded the streams, keeping the water cool for the young salmon. As settlers cleared these forests in order to create farmland and get lumber, they doomed the

Sheathed in ice, a loaded iron-ore barge passes through the Soo Locks into Lake Huron during a late-January storm. A fleet of icebreakers usually manages to keep the Great Lakes open to commercial shipping until February each winter; then subzero cold and heavy snowfalls often shut down lake traffic until the spring thaw in April.

Ten-foot-high breakers lash the lower floors of a luxury apartment building on Chicago's Lake Michigan shore during a brutal storm in April of 1973. Heavy rains, capping many months of above-average precipitation, caused millions of dollars' worth of property damage and raised the water level of all the Great Lakes to a 20-year high.

Atlantic salmon. The last salmon was pulled out of Lake Ontario in 1890.

The depletion of Ontario's Atlantic salmon set the stage for the subsequent struggles of deepwater fish to survive there and in the other Great Lakes. Two alien marine species began to appear in Ontario. These intruders were the alewife and the sea lamprey, both of them species that spawn in fresh-water streams but ordinarily spend their adult lives in the ocean.

The first of these invaders, noticed in Lake Ontario in 1873, was the alewife, a member of the herring family that probably reached the lake via the Hudson River, Erie Canal and Oswego River. As the salmon dwindled, the little alewife — less than nine inches long — thrived in Ontario, feeding on the eggs of other small fish and successfully competing for the available supply of zooplankton. In 20 years the alewife multiplied at an almost unbelievable rate and became one of the lake's dominant species.

In 1932 the completion of the Welland Canal, which linked Ontario and Erie while bypassing Niagara Falls, opened up new waters for the alewife to conquer. Alewives migrated westward into the other lakes, out-competing native species for food. Populations of small planktivores, such as the herring, emerald shiner, yellow perch, deepwater cisco and deepwater sculpin, began to decline. Alewives were first noticed in Lake Huron in 1951; less than two decades later, they made up 99 per cent of that lake's commercial fish harvest. By the early 1970s, they represented about half of the fish catch in the entire Great Lakes.

The advent of the alewife dismayed commercial fishermen, who found the species less valuable than other small fish. The alewife is also a nuisance to lakeside residents. Periodically, enormous numbers of alewives die off at once, for reasons unknown, paving the beaches with decomposing corpses.

The second intruder into the Great Lakes was an equally serious menace, especially to the lakes' population of large fish. The eel-like sea lamprey is a

fearsome parasite. It grows to nearly two feet in length and feeds by attaching a sucker-like mouth to the skin of the prey, rasping it with horny teeth and then drawing out the blood and other internal fluids. The lamprey's favorite prey are large firm-bodied fish, such as lake trout and whitefish — species that, ironically, might have slowed the proliferation of the alewife.

The lamprey appeared in Ontario in significant numbers almost immediately after the alewife and most likely followed the alewife's route up the Hudson and the Erie Canal to the Oswego River. The lamprey, too, benefited from the absence of the Atlantic salmon, reproducing rapidly in the warmth of the same tributary streams where too much silt and too little shade had made conditions untenable for the hatching of salmon eggs.

The lamprey's parasitic nature enabled it to move into the other Great Lakes more quickly than the alewife after the completion of the Welland Canal in 1932. While the free-swimming alewife had to struggle upstream through the canal locks, lampreys apparently got a free ride, attaching their suction-cup mouth to larger fish.

Migrating ever westward, the lamprey reached Lake Superior by 1950. With virtually no natural enemies present, it proliferated, feasting upon trout and whitefish. In combination with unregulated commercial fishing, the lamprey devastated native stocks. In a decade, Lake Huron's commercial whitefish catch dropped from 3.5 million pounds to 100,000 pounds. Lake Michigan's harvest of trout plummeted from 6.5 million pounds to zero.

Thousands of alewife carcasses litter the shores of the Great Lakes in 1967. These massive die-offs, believed to be caused largely by overpopulation, have diminished since naturalists began stocking the Great Lakes with lake trout, salmon and other alewife predators.

The lamprey also contributed to the success of the alewife. Ordinarily, trout and other large predators would have controlled the alewife population, but these predators had become the prey of the bloodthirsty lamprey.

Long after creating favorable conditions for the invasions of the alewife and lamprey, human beings attempted to restore ecological balance to the lakes. During the early 1950s, U.S. and Canadian scientists launched a series of counterattacks to control the lamprey's propagation in the tributaries. They installed barriers of electrically charged wires to block the streams and prevent spawning. But this method brought only partial success, for in times of high water, the lamprey simply swam over the wires.

Far more effective was a selective toxicant to kill the larvae of lamprey. The U.S. Fish and Wildlife Service's Hammond Bay Laboratory on Lake Michigan developed the lampricide after testing more than 4,000 chemicals. When carefully applied, it proved fatal to young lampreys in the spawning streams yet had little or no adverse effect on other species.

Between 1958 and 1972, the lamprey-producing tributaries of all the lakes but Erie, which was less seriously affected, were treated with the new chemical. The result was a dramatic decline in the lamprey population. In Lake Superior alone, two treatments of the tributaries reduced the number of adult lampreys by no less than 90 per cent.

Meanwhile, fishery managers supplemented this successful control program by restocking the lamprey-depleted supply of lake trout and whitefish with hatchery fish. With the lamprey under control, both species flourished. In some areas of intensive stocking, the trout actually surpassed its prelamprey abundance by the late 1960s.

Unfortunately, the sharp reduction in lamprey did not end the problem altogether; it increased the fitness of the species to survive. Relieved of the stresses of overpopulation, lamprey now grow faster and larger. Even more ominous is the fact that adult females now produce more eggs. Clearly, the program of lampricide must be continued for the foreseeable future.

For the counterattack against the alewife, biologists used other intruders. In 1966, they started introducing stocks of certain salmonids that were also alien to the Great Lakes but could be counted upon to consume

Two lampreys *(right)* drain a carp's vital fluids. The lamprey's mouth *(above)* clamps onto the fish, while rasps on the parasite's tongue bore into the fish's flesh and expose it to draining suction. A two-and-a-half-pound lamprey will destroy more than 30 pounds of fish in 18 months.

large quantities of the unwanted alewife. The Pacific coho salmon was stocked in Lake Michigan; chinook salmon and steelhead trout were later introduced to several of the lakes.

The populations of these salmonids have to be sustained by continual stocking, because they do not reproduce successfully in the lake tributaries. But the stocking has paid off by substantially cutting the overabundance of alewives. It has also provided a bonus: Salmonids gorging on alewives quickly grow to considerable size and attract increasing numbers of sportsmen eager for a prize catch. In fact, sport fishing has surpassed commercial fishing on the Great Lakes.

Over the years, other new species have been established in the lakes by human design or accident, among them the rainbow smelt, the carp and the pink salmon. But efforts to restore the native Atlantic salmon to Lake Ontario have failed. In the span of less than a century, the Great Lakes have changed so rapidly under human influence that this species apparently no longer can survive in any of these sweet-water oceans.

Even the oldest plant and animal species in the Great Lakes have had only a few thousand years to become adapted to their environment. By contrast, the flora and fauna of Lake Baikal have gone through millions of years of evolution and adaptation. There, the age of the lake, coupled with its isolation, has allowed nature, working at a leisurely pace, to permit new forms to evolve and alien intruders to adapt without sudden shocks to the delicate web of aquatic life.

Largely as a result, the biology of Baikal is unique. No fewer than 1,700 species of plants and animals inhabit its clear, cold waters. More than two thirds of them — including a fresh-water seal — are found nowhere else.

Baikal has another characteristic that contributes importantly to its rich diversity of plants and animals: the lake's extraordinary depth. Baikal is only 395 miles long and 30 miles wide on the average and thus has only about 40 per cent of Lake Superior's surface area. But it occupies the world's deepest continental trench and has waters extending downward to 5,314 feet, about four times the depth of Superior. Baikal holds four fifths of all the standing fresh water in the Soviet Union.

The mighty tectonic forces that shaped Baikal began about 80 million years ago in the late Mesozoic era, when dinosaurs still stalked the region. What had once been a broad basin of marshes and shallow lakes with a subtropical climate was shaken and reshaped by tremendous vertical shifts in the earth's crust. As the region quivered with earthquake after earthquake, huge blocks were thrust upward as mountains. Other blocks of the crust subsided, forming deep valleys and the great rift that now constitutes the steep-walled basin of Baikal.

Perhaps 25 million years ago, the waters came pouring into the basin. They flowed through the valleys formed by the tectonic forces and also carved new ones. Today, a total of 336 rivers and streams flow into Baikal, draining an area of 208,494 square miles — or 13 per cent more than the drainage area of all the Great Lakes together. Half of all the water entering Baikal comes from the 700-mile-long Selenga River, which drains northern Mongolia. Baikal's sole outlet is the Angara River; it flows north into the mighty 2,364-mile-long Yenisei, which discharges into the Arctic Ocean.

It is mainly melting snow from the mountains that determines seasonal

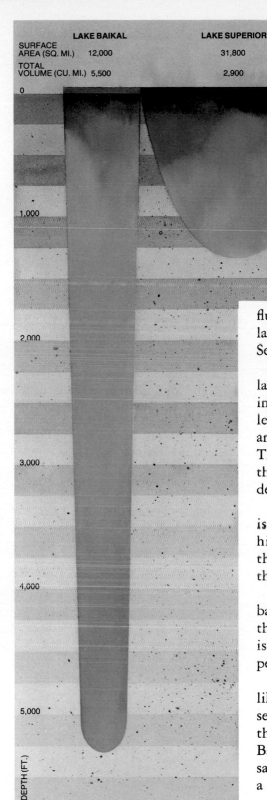

	LAKE BAIKAL	LAKE SUPERIOR	LAKE MICHIGAN	LAKE HURON	LAKE ERIE	LAKE ONTARIO
SURFACE AREA (SQ. MI.)	12,000	31,800	22,300	23,000	9,910	7,340
TOTAL VOLUME (CU. MI.)	5,500	2,900	1,180	850	116	393

These sketches show in cross section the relative surface area and depth of Siberia's Lake Baikal and the five Great Lakes. Baikal has only half the surface area of Lake Superior, but because it is roughly four times as deep (not counting its silt-filled abyss), it contains as much water as all the Great Lakes combined. The six lakes together hold 40 per cent of all the fresh water in the world.

fluctuations in Baikal's water level. In these frigid climes, the thaw comes late. The water-level lows occur in March and April. By the peak month of September, the level has risen two or three feet.

Such fluctuations are minor compared with those that occurred over the lake's long history. Terraces on the slopes of mountainous islands in the lake indicate that the water once stood at least 650 feet higher than its current level. And geologists have found sediments deposited at the mouths of ancient tributaries nearly 2,200 feet below the present surface of the lake. The wide shifts in water levels may have been caused by the freezing and thawing of glaciers or by an increased outflow of water resulting from the deepening of the Angara outlet.

Majestic evidence of the tectonic forces that gave birth to Baikal exists around the lake and within it. Mountain ranges up to 6,000 feet high border the lake. Beneath its surface stand two submerged ridges that cut across the width of the lake and separate the Baikal trench into three distinct basins.

A range called the Akademichesky forms the northern edge of the central basin of Lake Baikal and rises nearly a mile from the bottom. A portion of the Akademichesky breaks through the surface of the lake and creates the island of Olkhon, which comprises 322 square miles and is capped by a peak 2,624 feet high.

Other features suggest that the region's turbulent geological pattern is likely to continue. Hot springs flowing into the lake bespeak underlying seismic activity. Thirty major earthquakes have shaken the region during the past two centuries. One of these quakes, in 1861, fractured a plain on Baikal's eastern shore so severely that more than 70 square miles of terrain sank. Baikal's waters rushed in, drowning about 1,300 people and creating a shallow new arm of the lake called Proval Bay.

Some scientists foresee even more cataclysmic results. They suggest that the Baikal trench is part of an immense rift system extending from well northeast of the lake to the southern extremity of the Caspian Sea and that this rift will gradually deepen, widen and elongate. The resulting schism, they believe, would be so vast that it would split eastern Asia into two distinct land masses. Thus Baikal would one day become a new ocean separating two new continents.

Like the Great Lakes, Baikal is already oceanic in several ways. It has waves more than 15 feet high during storms, and its waters moderate temperatures in the surrounding areas. In June, temperatures seldom exceed

64° F. around the lake, but at the city of Irkutsk, 36 miles to the north, the thermometer often reaches 86° F. In winter, temperatures in Baikal's valley typically remain about 17° F. higher than in Irkutsk. Of course, Baikal is cold indeed, often plunging to −60° F. By February or March, a blanket of ice more than six feet thick covers the entire lake, and the spring breakup of ice cover comes late — during May in the south and often not until early June in the north.

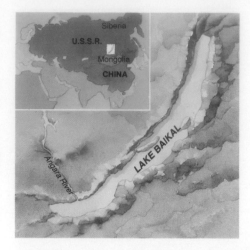

All through the winter, however, new life is stirring beneath the ice, which is startlingly clear at whatever thickness. Sunlight passes through the ice, allowing reproduction of microscopic plant life. This microfloral bloom occurs within about 30 feet of the surface of the water. Zooplankters, such as rotifers and copepods, gather in thick swarms as they feed on the phytoplankton.

Because of its size and vigorous circulation patterns, Baikal is rich enough in oxygen to sustain life even at its greatest depths. The most important factors affecting its flora and fauna are the spatial and seasonal distribution of warmth and sunlight. The annual breakup of the ice brings abrupt change in the surface layers of the lake: rising temperatures, surface turbulence caused by the clash of cold water and warm air, and sunlight that penetrates 150 feet or more. Spring algae and zooplankton slowly disperse downward and die, and by July, other types of phytoplankton, especially blue-green algae, flourish in the uppermost water.

Zooplankton grazes here in the summer, along with the small fish and other organisms that consume phytoplankton. In the wake of the zooplankters rise the large predators — but only at certain times of day.

The feeding patterns of one such predator, the salmon-like omul, have been studied in detail by Mikhail Kozhov, a zoologist at the State University of Irkutsk. Kozhov kept young omuls in large round tanks and observed their behavior in all seasons and at all hours. He found that the fish were largely inactive until water temperatures reached summer levels, typically about 54° to 60° F. in the top 13 feet of Baikal. Even then, they moved little during the bright of day or dark of night. At twilight, however, the omuls gathered in a school and moved rapidly, feeding intensely from about 6 to 9 p.m. and again around dawn.

Kozhov explains that the omuls search for food by sight. Their prey, scattered during the daytime, rise and graze on phytoplankton at night, when poor visibility protects them from omuls and other predators. At dusk and dawn, however, the dim light is sufficient for the omuls to find their prey and feed on them. "What is taking place here," observes Kozhov in conclusion, "is a two-way process of accommodation to the biotic conditions of life. The prey develops means of escaping destruction, while the consumer perfects the means of finding food."

Biologists tend to divide Baikal's habitats into three major depth zones. In the shallow coastal waters no deeper than 60 or 70 feet live plants and animals that, for the most part, are also found in other Siberian lakes.

Interesting exceptions to this general rule are several species of caddis flies that are found in no other lake. They have adapted to Baikal's turbulent surface by evolving small wings that are more like paddles, along with legs modified for swimming and hairy bodies that give them buoyancy. They mate and deposit eggs in the water or swim to shore and lay eggs there. Most remarkable is the fact that evolution has robbed them of the

The map at left shows Lake Baikal wedged between mountain ranges 50 miles from the border of Mongolia. The lake is fed by 336 tributaries but has only one outlet, the Angara River *(lower left)*, a tributary of the Yenisei, which flows north to the Arctic Ocean.

The port of Kultuk, on Lake Baikal's southern shore, lies on the Trans-Siberian Railroad at the foot of mile-high mountains of the Khamar-Daban range. Kultuk is a shipping point for building materials and other bulk goods destined for settlements around the lake.

ability to fly. Flying apparently was less of an asset than the ability to swim, especially when adult caddis flies emerged and attempted to reach shore over Baikal's wind-roiled surface.

But most of the species of plant and animal life that are unique to Lake Baikal exist in its deeper waters — in the intermediate zone that extends down to 660 feet and in the deep abyssal zone underneath that. As the depth increases, life-forms found elsewhere in Siberia disappear and are replaced by native organisms that have evolved in response to the special conditions in Baikal. In these two zones, more than 80 per cent of the species are endemic Baikalians.

In the deepest waters, where the temperature hovers near 38° F. throughout the year, light never penetrates, and hence many of the species here have little or no eyesight. For example, some of the abyssal Baikalian amphipods — small crustaceans with many-segmented bodies and seven pairs of

thoracic legs — have only indentations on the sides of their heads where there once were eyes; these amphipods orient themselves with the aid of exceptionally long antennae.

The waters of Baikal are home to no fewer than 50 species of fish, half of them endemic to the lake. The largest species is the lake sturgeon, which sometimes reaches 10 feet in length and can weigh more than 500 pounds. Valued for both its succulent flesh and its large quantities of caviar, the sturgeon for years was so overfished that it almost disappeared. Stringent limitations on catching the fish have recently brought it back to abundance.

Baikal's main commercial species is the omul. A member of the salmonid family, the adult omul is a foot long and weighs up to nine pounds. When the fish is hauled from the icy waters, it sometimes emits a piercing cry as air is expelled from its swim bladder. Siberians say of anyone who whines and complains, "He cries like an omul."

Other fish with bizarre characteristics thrive in Baikal. Among the strangest are two endemic subgroups of the species known to Siberians as the golomyanka. This scaleless fish grows to a maximum length of eight inches and contains so much body oil — a third or more by weight — that it is translucent. At night it rises to the surface to feed on amphipods and other zooplankton. But the golomyanka cannot linger long at the surface: It is so adapted to the cold that temperatures much above 45° F. prove fatal. When the dead golomyanka washes ashore, its fat melts away in the sun, leaving little but skin and bones.

Equally as strange is the golomyanka's method of reproduction. Instead of laying eggs, the adult female fish gives birth to live larvae. A female

Silhouetted against Lake Baikal's frozen expanse, local residents cross thick ice on horse-drawn sleds. Late in the Siberian winter, paths etched straight across the ice replace winding mountain roads through the region.

The nerpa seal, one of two fresh-water seals in the world, is unique to Lake Baikal. Nerpa seals survive the winter freeze by making air holes through the ice as it forms and keeping the holes open all through the winter months; their pups are born during February and March on the frozen surface of the lake.

produces about 2,000 progeny in the autumn, but she often fails to survive the process; it is common for the mother golomyanka's belly to burst during childbirth.

The omul and the golomyanka are favorite foods of Baikal's only aquatic mammal, the nerpa seal. A rare fresh-water seal, the nerpa inhabits rocky crags on the northeastern edge of the lake in summer and migrates south with the advance of the ice in early winter. The waters of Baikal are so clear that submerged nerpa seals can be seen and counted by scientists hovering overhead in a helicopter. An aerial survey recently set Baikal's population of these unique mammals at more than 25,000.

The closest relative of the nerpa seal lives nearly 2,000 miles away in the salty Arctic Ocean, the original habitat of the omul salmon. The presence of these two outsiders suggested to some scientists that Baikal may once have been a part of the Arctic Ocean. But now there is general agreement that the nerpa, as well as the omul, somehow reached Lake Baikal indirectly, struggling upstream for hundreds of miles by way of the Yenisei and Angara Rivers. Recently discovered geological evidence indicates that the trip was then considerably shorter, for the Arctic Ocean formerly extended much farther inland.

According to Grigor I. Galazii, director of the Limnological Institute of the U.S.S.R. Academy of Sciences, the nerpa ancestor's journey from the Arctic Ocean may have occurred as recently as 12,000 years ago. In that relatively brief time, this salt-water seal adapted to the new conditions of a lake and evolved into the nerpa, a new species that zoologists have labeled *Phoca sibirica*. Although the Arctic seal and its descendant have similar flipper structure and harbor identical internal and external parasites, the nerpa shows distinct changes, such as color. The nerpa has silvery gray fur, while the Arctic seal is yellow with black marks. Galazii describes the nerpa as "a good example of the creation of a new species in a very short time."

A major reason for the abundance of life in Baikal is the absence of pollution in its waters, which rank among the cleanest on earth. But even though the lake is remote from major population centers, it is endangered by industrial waste, which has accompanied the Soviet government's development of Siberia. Three cellulose-manufacturing facilities planned for Baikal's southern shore and for the tributary Selenga River threatened to contaminate the lake with effluents that, despite treatment by up-to-date filtration systems, contain phenols and other toxic nonbiodegradable chemicals. As a result of protests led by the Soviet Academy of Sciences, two of the proposed factories were eliminated and the third redesigned to curtail water pollution.

According to an alert issued by the academy in 1977, chemical pollution threatened the most vital zooplankter in Baikal's food chain, the tiny crustacean Epischura. This creature, like the lake's other endemic life-forms, evolved under conditions of exceptional water purity. Even relatively slight changes in water chemistry, the report warned, might spell disaster for the Epischura. The report concluded that the lake was on the brink of irreversible destructive changes.

In issuing this stern warning, Soviet scientists undoubtedly had in mind the familiar degradation suffered by the Great Lakes. They knew that not much more than a century earlier, the water in the five Great Lakes had been as clean and clear as that of Baikal — "so pristine," one writer noted, "that it was all but distilled."

Like Baikal, all the Great Lakes originally possessed the desirable oligotrophic qualities of being oxygen-rich and nutrient-poor. Offshore, the microscopic phytoplankton that serve as the basis for the food chain consisted mostly of diverse diatoms that were well adapted to cold water and low levels of the nutrient phosphorus.

But the by-products of human activities have altered the chemistry of the Great Lakes through two general types of pollution. Excess nutrients have overfertilized the lakes, accelerating the natural aging process of eutrophication that eventually brings death to a lake by causing excessive plant production. And pollution by man-made toxic chemicals has posed a direct and immediate threat to the existence of fish and other aquatic life.

Core samples taken from the bottom of Superior have revealed that the lake took a dramatic turn for the worse around 1890, with a tenfold increase in sediments. Human activity was increasing in the American Midwest. People were clearing forests, fertilizing farms, building industries, dumping wastes — and the lakes were beginning to show it.

In the past half century, all of the Great Lakes have shown evidence of increasing eutrophication brought on by pollution. Nutrients, such as nitrogen and phosphorus from wastes and from the runoff of fertilized farm fields, nourish the growth of nuisance algae that deplete the supply of oxygen and cause rapid changes in the aquatic ecosystem. Only Superior can still be considered chemically oligotrophic.

The most polluted and hence most eutrophic of the lakes is Erie. It has the largest population (13 million people) in its drainage basin, the great-

The Rainfall That Kills

The misty beauty of Lake Colden, high in New York's Adirondack Mountains, masks its fate as a victim of acid rain. Once a mecca for trout fishermen, Colden's acidic waters have been empty of fish since 1970.

"The trouble with acid rain is that you can't see it." So laments a ranger in New York's Adirondack Mountains, where more than 200 of the region's 2,800 lakes have succumbed to acidic precipitation and hundreds more are in danger.

Indeed, the rain and snow that fall poisonously on the Adirondacks give no visible warning of the lethal burden they carry: solutions of sulfur dioxide and nitrogen oxides resulting from combustion of coal, oil and natural gas hundreds of miles upwind in the industrialized Midwest. Moreover, affected lakes rarely appear to be contaminated until it is too late. On the contrary, their waters turn pristinely clear — because the suspended bits of plankton and decaying matter that can give healthy water a murky look have been eliminated.

Yet one telltale clue does reveal the moribund condition of an acidic lake: its silence. The bullfrogs and loons and buzzing flies are gone. So are most or all of the lake's fish.

The Adirondacks are especially vulnerable because their granitic watersheds contain little lime, which could act as an alkaline buffer to neutralize toxic fallout. But lakes and streams across a wide band of the Northern Hemisphere are in similar danger. In eastern Canada, more than 2,000 lakes have become so acidified that they cannot support trout or bass. Norway and Sweden have become a dumping ground for acid in rain, snow, fog and even solid particles carried north on prevailing winds from industrialized Europe.

Belatedly, acid contamination has been recognized as a problem requiring international cooperation to lower toxic emissions at their source. Ecologists, meanwhile, are taking stopgap measures (*overleaf*) to slow the decline of threatened waters into deathly silence.

A researcher tests the chemical balance of Woods Lake in Adirondack Park during the spring melt of acid-contaminated snow. The lake once sustained thousands of plant and animal species; only a few acid-resistant species remain.

A Swedish ecologist lifts a hand smeared with polluted muck from a lake where windborne fog had deposited toxic particles from industrial nations to the south. One fifth of Sweden's 100,000 lakes suffer from acid contamination; in 4,000 of them, fish have died out completely.

Caged brook trout succumb to acid poisoning in a mountain stream. The fish were part of an ongoing attempt to breed an acid-tolerant trout.

A lake in Sweden gets a heavy injection of lime to neutralize its acidity. Such treatment has proved only temporarily effective.

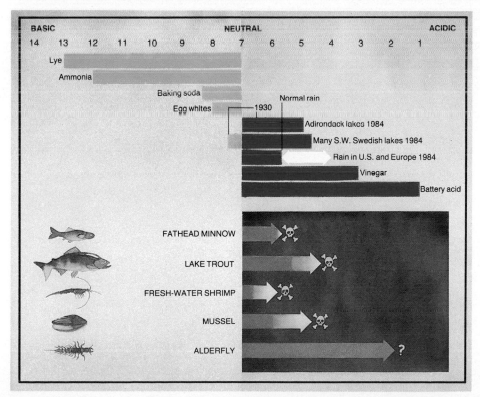

BASIC						NEUTRAL							ACIDIC
14	13	12	11	10	9	8	7	6	5	4	3	2	1

Lye
Ammonia
Baking soda
Egg whites — 1930
Normal rain
Adirondack lakes 1984
Many S.W. Swedish lakes 1984
Rain in U.S. and Europe 1984
Vinegar
Battery acid

FATHEAD MINNOW
LAKE TROUT
FRESH-WATER SHRIMP
MUSSEL
ALDERFLY ?

Scientists measure chemical balance on a pH scale, which assigns the highest numbers to such alkaline substances as lye and ammonia, and the lowest to the most acidic, such as battery acid and vinegar. Distilled water, which is chemically neutral, is rated pH 7. The pH values are logarithmic: A substance rated pH 5 is 10 times as acidic as one rated pH 6. Normal rain contains some carbonic acid and is rated pH 5.6. Any precipitation that has a lower pH rating is defined as acid rain. The arrows on the lower chart show the levels at which various aquatic species resist water acidity *(dark orange)* before they begin to suffer reproductive failure *(light orange)* and die off.

est concentration of industrial activity along its shores and the least volume of water (116 cubic miles) to dilute the chemicals pouring in. By the early 1960s, Erie had become so polluted that the press pronounced it dead.

Reports of its death were both premature and ironic, for Erie's problem was too much life of the wrong kind. The principal culprit was the inflow of phosphorus, which stimulates the growth of phytoplankton. In 25 years, the amount of phosphorus in Erie's western waters had nearly tripled, and the production of phyloplankton had increased manyfold. All this growth depleted the supply of other nutrients, such as silicon, which is essential for the development of diatoms. These minute forms of algae, a critical part of the food chain, soon dwindled.

At the same time, blue-green algae began to proliferate, because this type of phytoplankton does not require silicon for growth. Blue-green algae's competitive advantage over the diatoms was further enhanced as increased inflows of phosphorus reduced the level of nitrogen in the water. Since blue-green algae can utilize nitrogen from the air and the diatoms must get theirs from the water, blue-green algae won out, and its great noxious blooms blanketed the lake.

The ascendancy of blue-green algae was unfortunate for a number of reasons. Most species are poor food sources for zooplankton, and some are actually toxic to other organisms. The algae smell bad and give the water a disagreeable taste. Large masses of algae shut off the sunlight and prevent this life-sustaining energy from reaching deeper waters.

Worst of all, when these algal masses die off in October and November, they sink to the bottom and decay. The decomposition absorbs oxygen from the water, making the oxygen unavailable for vital life processes. In the part of Erie first blighted by burgeoning blue-green algae — its shallow western basin — declining oxygen levels virtually wiped out the rich bottom fauna of mussels, caddis flies, midges and burrowing mayflies. The bottom is now the habitat of undesirable species of worms and small mollusks.

Similar effects occurred in Erie's deeper and larger central basin. In the past, the basin's deepest waters were a vital summer refuge for such cold-water fish as lake trout, whitefish, herring and blue pike. But decaying algae used up the oxygen, and by 1973, samplings showed that 94 per cent of the deep water was anoxic — dangerously deficient in oxygen. Erie's small eastern basin, which averages 80 feet in depth, has received less sediment and fewer nutrients than the other basins; it continues to sustain populations of a few oligotrophic species, such as opossum shrimp.

The changes wrought by too much phosphorus — together with other environmental stresses, such as the invasion of the sea lamprey and overfishing — brought about the biological extinction of blue pike and the virtual extinction of Erie's lake trout, whitefish and herring. Though the total commercial harvest on Erie has remained relatively constant at about 50 million pounds per year, the kinds of fish caught and their worth have changed drastically. Catches now are dominated by warm-water species, such as yellow perch, white bass, smelt, carp, goldfish and fresh-water drum — most of which have low market value.

The decline in the Erie fishery reinforced other alarming evidence of pollution — beaches that had to be shut down, windrows of decaying algae on the shores, slime-covered waters. Newspaper headlines, along with public and political concern, had the salutary effect of bringing increased research funds to limnologists and biologists studying the Great Lakes.

Their findings are leading scientists to be cautiously optimistic about the prospects for reversing Erie's eutrophic trend. Water turns over much more rapidly in Erie than in any of the other Great Lakes: Its flushing time is only three years compared with much longer cycles in some of the other lakes. If the water entering Erie can be cleaned up, enormous progress could be made in perhaps only a decade or two.

The task of reducing phosphorus inflow is far from insuperable. Since 40 per cent of the phosphorus entering Lake Erie comes from the phosphates used as softening agents in laundry detergents, the U.S. ban on phosphate detergents in 1972 had a tremendous impact, reducing the phosphates entering the lake to 6,700 tons in 1975 and 2,700 in 1981. In turn, reduction of phosphates in Erie has helped improve the condition of Lake Ontario, which receives half of its pollutants in the water flow from Erie. At the same time, phosphates entering Ontario from industrial and sewage-treatment plants in its own basin declined by a third in less than a decade —from an estimated 16,500 tons in 1972 to about 11,000 tons in 1980.

While phosphorus and other plant nutrients alter the chemistry of the water and hence reshape the ecosystem, they are not in themselves directly harmful to aquatic life. Perhaps more serious is a second kind of pollution: man-made chemicals and heavy metals such as mercury and lead, which can prove directly poisonous to any organism. No fewer than 400 potentially toxic substances have been found in the Great Lakes; topping the list is dioxin, which is about 10,000 times as poisonous as cyanide. These contaminants come from every imaginable source. Some flow into the lakes in the effluents from industrial and sewage-treatment plants. Pesticides and herbicides run off from farmland. Other harmful substances are deposited in the water from the atmosphere, especially such by-products of fossil-fuel combustion as lead from automobile exhausts and cadmium and mercury from factory smokestacks.

Though the contaminants found in the Great Lakes are present in minute amounts, they become concentrated in the food chain in proportionately higher quantities. Since the late 1960s, concentrations of various chemicals have periodically reached such high levels in trout, salmon and other fish that some members of those species have been deemed unsafe for human consumption. In 1969, for example, in Lake Michigan, the culprit was the pesticide DDT, the production of which was later barred in both the United States and Canada. In 1976, in Lake Ontario, it was mirex, a chlorinated hydrocarbon used as a pesticide and as a flame retardant.

A relatively recent addition to the roster of dangerous substances is polychlorinated biphenyls (PCBs), widely used in paints, printing ink and insecticides. PCBs, perhaps more than any other classes of synthetic chemicals, illustrate dramatically how contaminants insinuate their way into the aquatic food web through a process known as bioconcentration. Small fish ingest the chemical by eating zooplankton that already have taken in PCBs by grazing upon contaminated phytoplankton. But because PCBs dissolve more readily in lipids (fats) than in water, fish also absorb the chemical as they breathe through their gills, which in part consist of lipids. The PCBs ingested by the fish are then permanently stored in their body fat. Thus a small bluegill, for example, can accumulate a concentration of PCBs many times greater than that in the surrounding water. Bioconcentration then

A thick scum from household and industrial detergents blankets the Olona River northwest of Milan. The river, which flows through Italy's major manufacturing region, also contains less visible but more dangerous toxins from the textile, tanning and chemical factories lining its banks. The entire area has been targeted by the government for a massive cleanup project.

proceeds up the food chain to the large predator fish and perhaps to human beings, with each link assimilating ever higher proportions of the toxin.

Research has demonstrated the deadly effects. In one experiment, mink that were fed coho salmon containing PCB concentrations of 10 parts per million showed a mortality rate of 71 per cent. Mink that were fed a diet containing 5 parts per million survived but ceased to reproduce. The effects on humans are uncertain, but the evidence suggests that PCBs interfere with prenatal development and may be carcinogenic.

A major step toward solution of the problem came in 1979, when regulations went into effect prohibiting the production of PCBs in the United States. But old PCBs still get into the lakes, more than half of them carried through the air from the burning of papers and other materials containing the chemicals. PCBs do decompose, but the process takes time. By the most optimistic estimate, PCBs will continue to threaten aquatic life for at least 20 years after the chemicals stop entering the Great Lakes.

Owing to their sheer size and proximity to so many people, the Great Lakes represent the problem of pollution writ large. But as the problems of Lake Baikal suggest, human contamination goes on in practically every lake and stream, no matter how remote from centers of population and industry.

In recent years, a new threat has been added to the list of problems endangering fresh-water ecosystems: acid rain. The two acids involved, sulfuric and nitric, build up inside clouds when droplets of water react with emissions of sulfur dioxide and nitrogen oxide, two familiar by-products of fossil-fuel combustion in autos and industry. Then the acids rain down on rivers and lakes and their basins, turning the water vinegary.

Hundreds of lakes in northern Europe, Canada and the northeastern United States have been blighted by acid rain. In addition to killing the zooplankton, plants and insects that fish feed on, acid rain compounds the problem by leaching out toxic metals from surrounding soils. In some small mountain lakes in the northeastern United States, acid rain has unleashed sufficient quantities of aluminum to exterminate entire populations of prized brook trout.

Such horror stories are all too commonplace. But, thanks largely to mounting public pressure against pollution, programs have been launched to cure many sick lakes and rivers. A fair number of these programs have produced encouraging results.

Small and medium-sized lakes are more quickly polluted than large ones but have proved easier to bring back to health. A prime example is Lake Washington, near the city of Seattle. By 1963, phosphorus in the effluents from 11 sewage-treatment plants had nourished stifling masses of blue-green algae that were accelerating the lake's demise through eutrophication. The algae had multiplied 12-fold in just 13 years.

Prodded by public protests against the smelly and unsightly algae, officials in 1963 began diverting the effluents into Puget Sound, eight miles from the lake. A secondary sewage-treatment plant was built on the shore of the sound to neutralize the added waste from the lake. The process was completed in 1968 and it reduced the phosphorus entering the lake by 82 per cent. By 1975, Lake Washington had effectively recovered from its bout with eutrophication.

Smaller lakes have been restored by various ingenious methods. In Green

Michael Faraday, the illustrious British physicist, presents his calling card to a malodorous Father Thames in this 1855 *Punch* cartoon. Following a river journey earlier that year, Faraday had written an angry letter to *The Times* of London, calling the river "an opaque brown fluid" in which "the feculence rolled up on clouds so dense that they were visible at the surface." His letter poured fuel on an already burning public issue: The Thames, which carried tons of toxic industrial pollution and untreated human waste, had been responsible for two outbreaks of cholera in which more than 14,000 people died.

Lake, also near Seattle, the concentration of nutrients was reduced by introducing a new and cleaner source of water into the lake, thus speeding the rate at which the lake's volume is replaced. In several lakes, undesirable nutrients have been removed by applying a chemical precipitant, such as calcium or ferric chloride, that combines with the phosphates to form insoluble compounds. The mixture settles to the bottom, carrying the algae with it and preventing the recirculation of the nutrients from the sediment.

Scientists applied a simple solution to the stubborn pollution of tiny Lake Trummen in southern Sweden. After diversion of effluents from the lake had failed to reverse eutrophication, limnologists decided the problem lay in the phosphate-saturated sediments on the shallow bottom. They attacked the lake bottom with a suction dredge and removed sediments more than a yard thick. This process quickly restored the lake's vitality.

Since rivers are constantly being flushed out by their running water, many have responded rapidly to cleanup campaigns. New York's Hudson River, pronounced "an open sewer" in the 1960s by a council of advisers to the U.S. President, improved enough under modest cleanup measures to attract long-absent sturgeon. The Willamette River in Oregon was until recently considered the most polluted river in the Pacific Northwest, but in just seven years it was freed of 90 per cent of its wastes.

Probably the most remarkable comeback of all has been staged by England's Thames River. As early as the 18th Century, surgeon-novelist Tobias Smollett wrote that the lower Thames was "composed of all the drugs, minerals, and poisons used in mechanics and manufacture." Conditions worsened as the area's population doubled and as a new invention, flush toilets, emptied wastes into the river instead of into cesspools. The decomposition of sewage consumed so much of the Thames's oxygen that the Atlantic salmon and other fish suffocated; only a few eels survived. Until three decades ago, the Thames was considered one of the worst-polluted bodies of water anywhere.

Under the goad of public indignation, strict new government standards finally were issued in the 1950s to curb the effluents being poured into the Thames. Sewage-treatment plants were progressively upgraded to limit oxygen-depleting nutrients, such as nitrogen and phosphorus. Mechanical aerators were installed in some places to mix oxygen into the water.

In three decades, this wide-ranging program of pollution control succeeded in reducing pollution in the Thames by an estimated 90 per cent. Gradually, the depleted levels of oxygen in the river began to rise. Measurements during the autumn of 1974 showed a dramatic increase in the proportion of dissolved oxygen from 10 to nearly 60 per cent.

The fish staged a comeback. The number of species thriving in the Thames swelled from that one eel species in 1950 to more than 100. The returnees included the long-departed Atlantic salmon, restocked from hatcheries beginning in 1979 and now increasing in the oxygen-enriched waters of the resurgent river.

The science of controlling and reversing pollution damage is still in its infancy. So too is the science of water management, which nations will need even more urgently as their populations continue to increase and to use more and more of the limited supply of fresh water. But present successes in conserving and rehabilitating at least some of the world's rivers and lakes offer distinct hope for the future of them all. Ω

Foraging swans swim in the Thames near a silo on the riverbank, their mere presence testifying to the success of the 20-year campaign to clean up the river. During the 1960s such birds had disappeared from the polluted river, which had no food to support them. As the cleanup progressed, aquatic plants and animals again became plentiful, and water birds returned in record numbers.

Glistening in the late-afternoon sun, the revitalized Thames River flows peacefully through rural Richmond, just eight miles upstream from London. After facing

death by pollution for seven centuries, the river was restored to health and beauty in little more than 20 years by a massive cleanup campaign.

ACKNOWLEDGMENTS

For their help with this volume, the editors thank: In **Australia**: Brisbane — Commonwealth Scientific and Industrial Research Organization. In **Austria**: Gosau — Reinhold Schmaranzer, Fremdenverkehrsverband Gosau. In **Canada**: Ontario — (Dorset) Dr. Ronald Hall, Ontario Ministry of the Environment. In **Great Britain**: London — Philippa Angrave, Francis Herbert, Royal Geographical Society; Derek Gregg, Thames Water Authority; Reading — N. J. Nicholson, Thames Water Authority; Sevenoaks — Dr. Pamela Harrison. In **Italy**: Milan — Maria Ceriotti, Marka; Lino Pellegrini; Luisa Ricciarini; Rome — Florita Botts, F.A.O. In the **Netherlands**: Amsterdam — Wayland R. Swain. In **Switzerland**: Dübendorf — Professor Heinz Ambühl, EAWAG; Geneva — Julia Faundez, W.H.O. In the

United States: California — (Davis) Dr. Peter C. Moyle, Wildlife and Fishery Biology, University of California; (Lee Vining) Jim Parker, the Mono Lake Committee; District of Columbia — Dr. Ernest A. Lachner, Marine and Freshwater Fisheries, Dr. Richard Vari, South American Fisheries, National Museum of Natural History; Florida — (Gainesville) Laurie Wilkins, Mammal Range, Florida State Museum; Michigan — (Ann Arbor) R. Stephen Schneider, Great Lakes and Marine Waters Center, The University of Michigan; Mississippi — (Vicksburg) Billy C. Bridges, U.S. Waterways Experiment Station; Herbert A. Kassner, U.S. Army Corps of Engineers; New York — (Buffalo) John A. Derbyshire, Thomas A. Wilkinson, U.S. Army Corps of Engineers; (New York) David and Anne

Doubilet; North Carolina — (Wilmington) Dr. Ralph W. Brauer, Director, Institute of Marine Biomedical Research, University of North Carolina; Pennsylvania — (Philadelphia) Dr. Frank Gill, Dr. Robert S. Ridgely, Academy of Natural Sciences of Philadelphia; Vermont — (Lyndonville) Dr. William H. Amos, Lyndon State College; Virginia — (Reston) Dr. Richard S. Williams Jr., U.S. Geological Survey; Washington — (Seattle) W. T. Edmondson, Department of Zoology, University of Washington. In **West Germany**: Cologne — Dr. Frank Kirschbaum, Zoologisches Institut, Universität Köln; Plön — Professor Jürgen Overbeck, Max-Planck-Institut für Limnologie.

The index was prepared by Barbara L. Klein.

BIBLIOGRAPHY

Books

Adams, George F., and Jerome Wyckoff, *Landforms*. New York: Golden Press, 1971.

Amos, William H.:
The Life of the Pond. New York: McGraw-Hill, 1967.
Wildlife of the Rivers. New York: Harry N. Abrams, 1981.

Angel, Heather, and Pat Wolseley, *The Water Naturalist*. New York: Facts On File, 1982.

Ault, Phil, *These Are the Great Lakes*. New York: Dodd, Mead, 1972.

Barton, Rita M., *Waterfalls of the World*. Truro, England: D. Bradford Barton, 1974.

Biswas, Asit K., *History of Hydrology*. Amsterdam: North Holland Publishing, 1970.

Boyer, Dwight:
Ships and Men of the Great Lakes. New York: Dodd, Mead, 1977.
True Tales of the Great Lakes. New York: Dodd, Mead, 1971.

Brander, Bruce, *The River Nile*. Washington: National Geographic Society, 1966.

Cavagnaro, David, *Living Water*. Palo Alto, Calif.: American West, 1971.

Coker, Robert E., *Streams, Lakes, Ponds*. Chapel Hill: The University of North Carolina Press, 1954.

Cole, Gerald A., *Textbook of Limnology*. St. Louis: The C. V. Mosby Company, 1983.

Credland, Peter, *The Living Earth: Rivers and Lakes*. The Danbury Press, 1975.

Czaya, Eberhard, *Rivers of the World*. New York: Van Nostrand Reinhold, 1981.

Davies, Delwyn, *Fresh Water: The Precious Resource*. New York: The Natural History Press, 1969.

Denton, George H., and Terence J. Hughes, eds., *The Last Great Ice Sheets*. New York: John Wiley & Sons, 1981.

Douglas, Gina, *The Ganges*. Morristown, N.J.: Silver Burdett, 1978.

Doxat, John, *The Living Thames: The Restoration of a Great Tidal River*. London: Hutchinson Benham, 1977.

Earnest, Don, *Aquatic Miniatures* (Wild, Wild World of Animals series). Amsterdam: Time-Life Films, 1979.

Edmondson, W. T., ed., *Fresh-Water Biology*. New York: John Wiley & Sons, 1963.

Ela, Jonathan, *The Faces of the Great Lakes*. San Francisco: Sierra Club Books, 1977.

Flint, Richard Foster, and Brian J. Skinner, *Physical Geology*. New York: John Wiley & Sons, 1977.

Frey, David G., ed., *Limnology in North America*. Madison: The University of Wisconsin Press, 1963.

Gaines, David, and the Mono Lake Committee, *Mono Lake Guidebook*. Lee Vining, Calif.: Kutsavi Books, 1981.

Gedzelman, Stanley David, *The Science and Wonders of the Atmosphere*. New York: John Wiley & Sons, 1980.

Goldman, Charles R., and Alexander J. Horne, *Limnology*. New York: McGraw-Hill, 1983.

Goulding, Michael, *The Fishes and the Forest: Explorations in Amazonian Natural History*. Berkeley: University of California Press, 1980.

Gregory, K. J., and D. E. Walling, eds., *Man and Environmental Processes: A Physical Geography Perspective*. Folkestone, England: Wm Dawson & Sons, 1979.

Gresswell, Dr. R. Kay, and Anthony Huxley, *Standard Encyclopedia of the World's Rivers and Lakes*. New York: Putnam, 1965.

Hamblin, W. Kenneth, *The Earth's Dynamic Systems: A Textbook in Physical Geology*. Minneapolis: Burgess, 1978.

Hope, Jack, *A River for the Living: The Hudson and Its People*. Barre, Mass.: Barre Publishing, 1975.

Hutchinson, G. Evelyn, *A Treatise on Limnology*. New York: John Wiley & Sons, 1957.

Hynes, H.B.N., *The Ecology of Running Waters*. Toronto: University of Toronto Press, 1970.

Jenkinson, Michael, *Wilderness Rivers of America*. New York: Harry N. Abrams, 1981.

Josephy, Alvin M., Jr., *The American Heritage Book of Natural Wonders*. New York: American Heritage, 1963.

Kozhov, Mikhail, *Lake Baikal and Its Life*. The Hague: Dr. W. Junk, 1963.

Lagler, Karl F., John E. Bardach and Robert R. Miller, *Ichthyology*. Ann Arbor: The University of Michigan, 1962.

Lane, Ferdinand C., *The World's Great Lakes*. Garden City, N.Y.: Doubleday, 1948.

Leopold, Luna B., *Water: A Primer*. San Francisco: W. H. Freeman, 1974.

Leopold, Luna B., M. Gordon Wolman and John P. Miller, *Fluvial Processes in Geomorphology*. San Francisco: W. H. Freeman, 1964.

Lerman, Abraham, ed., *Lakes: Chemistry, Geology, Physics*. New York: Springer-Verlag, 1978.

Lock, Maurice A., and D. Dudley Williams, eds., *Perspectives in Running Water Ecology*. New York: Plenum Press, 1981.

Ludman, Allan, *Physical Geology*. New York: McGraw-Hill, 1982.

Lurie, Edward, *Louis Agassiz: A Life in Science*. Chicago: The University of Chicago Press, 1960.

Moorehead, Alan:
The Blue Nile. New York: Harper & Row, 1962.

The White Nile. New York: Harper & Row, 1971.

Morisawa, Marie, *Streams: Their Dynamics and Morphology*. New York: McGraw-Hill, 1968.

Moss, Brian, *Ecology of Fresh Waters*. New York: John Wiley & Sons, 1980.

Nelson, Joseph S., *Fishes of the World*. New York: John Wiley & Sons, 1976.

O'Clery, Helen, *The Pegasus Book of the Nile*. London: Dennis Dobson, 1970.

Oglesby, Ray T., Clarence A. Carlson and James A. McCann, *River Ecology and Man*. New York: Academic Press, 1972.

Oldroyd, Harold, *The Natural History of Flies*. New York: W. W. Norton, 1965.

Our Continent: A Natural History of North America. Washington: National Geographic Society, 1976.

Pennak, Robert W., *Fresh-Water Invertebrates of the United States*. New York: John Wiley & Sons, 1978.

Press, Frank, and Raymond Siever, *Earth*. San Francisco: W. H. Freeman, 1978.

Rand McNally Encyclopedia of World Rivers. Chicago: Rand McNally, 1980.

Reader's Digest Natural Wonders of the World. New York: Reader's Digest Press, 1980.

Reeves, C. C., Jr., *Introduction to Paleolimnology*. Amsterdam: Elsevier, 1968.

Rousmaniere, John, *The Enduring Great Lakes*. New York: W. W. Norton, 1979.

Singh, Raghubir, *Ganga: Sacred River of India*. Hong Kong: The Perennial Press, 1974.

Sterba, Günther, *Freshwater Fishes of the World*. Transl. and rev. by Denys W. Tucker. New York: Viking, 1963.

Strahler, Arthur N., and Alan H. Strahler, *Elements of Physical Geography*. New York: John Wiley & Sons, 1979.

Tesmer, Irving H., ed., *Colossal Cataract: The Geologic History of Niagara Falls*. Albany: State University of New York Press, 1981.

Thomas, Bill, *American Rivers: A Natural History*. New York: W. W. Norton, 1978.

Thompson, Gerald, and Jennifer Coldrey, *The Pond*. Cambridge: The MIT Press, 1984.

Thomson, George Malcolm, *The Search for the Northwest Passage*. New York: Macmillan, 1975.

Twidale, C. R., *Analysis of Landforms*. New York: John Wiley & Sons, 1976.

Usinger, Robert L., *The Life of Rivers and Streams*. New York: McGraw-Hill, 1967.

Warren, Ruth, *The Nile: The Story of Pharaohs, Farmers and Explorers*. New York: McGraw-Hill, 1968.

Wetzel, Robert G., *Limnology*. New York: Saunders College Publishing, 1983.

Whitton, B. A., ed., *River Ecology*. Berkeley:

University of California Press, 1975.

Willock, Colin, and the Editors of Time-Life Books, *Africa's Rift Valley* (The World's Wild Places series). Amsterdam: Time-Life Books, 1974.

Worthington, E. Barton, *Rivers of the World: The Nile.* Morristown, N.J.: Silver Burdett, 1978.

Zumberge, James H., *Elements of Physical Geology.* New York: John Wiley & Sons, 1976.

Periodicals

"America the Dry." *Life*, July 1981.

Amos, William H., "Unseen Life of a Mountain Stream." *National Geographic*, April 1977.

Campbell, Robert:
  "The Interaction of Two Great Rivers Helps Sustain the Earth's Vital Biosphere." First of two parts. *Smithsonian*, September 1977.
  "A Timely Reprieve or a Death Sentence for the Amazon." Second of two parts. *Smithsonian*, October 1977.

Canby, Thomas Y., "Water: Our Most Precious Resource." *National Geographic*, August 1980.

Carlier, Jean, "Défendre le Baïkal Sacré." *GEO*, January 1983.

Chasan, Daniel Jack, "Mono Lake vs. Los Angeles: A Tug-of-war for Precious Water." *Smithsonian*, February 1981.

Chelminski, Rudolph, "Baikal Survives as a Prize for the Whole Planet." *Smithsonian*, November 1975.

"The Colossus of Brazil." *GEO*, November 1981.

Conger, Dean, "Siberia: Russia's Frozen Frontier." *National Geographic*, March 1967.

Craig, J. F., "A Study of the Food and Feeding of Perch, *Perca Fluviatilis L.*, in Windermere." *Freshwater Biology*, 1978.

Cummins, Kenneth W., "Structure and Function of Stream Ecosystems." *BioScience*, Vol. 24, No. 11, no date.

Domning, Daryl P., "Marching Teeth of the Manatee." *Natural History*, May 1983.

Elster, Hans-Joachim, "History of Limnology." *International Association of Theoretical and Applied Limnology* (Stuttgart), June 1974.

"The Epic Tale of Itaipu." *Manchete* (Rio de Janeiro), 1982.

Findley, Rowe, "The Bittersweet Waters of the Lower Colorado." *National Geographic*, October 1973.

Fittkau, E. J., "Role of Caimans in the Nutrient Regime of Mouth-Lakes of Amazon Affluents: An Hypothesis." *Biotropica* (Lawrence, Kans.), 1970.

George, Uwe, "Birth of an Ocean." *GEO*, July 1978.

Gottsberger, Gerhard, "Seed Dispersal by Fish in the Inundated Regions of Humaitá, Amazonia." *Biotropica* (Lawrence, Kans.), 1978.

Green, Timothy, "Father Thames Has Cleaned Up His Act at Long Last." *Smithsonian*, May 1978.

Gregory, K. J., "Why Rivers Change Their Course." *The Geographical Magazine*, March 1984.

Hall, Stephen S., "The Bird World's Ace Fisher." *GEO*, March 1982.

Hauser, Hillary, "Exploring a Sunken Realm in Australia." *National Geographic*, January 1984.

Hendrey, George R., "Acid Rain and Gray Snow." *Natural History*, February 1981.

Hutchinson, G. Evelyn, "Eutrophication." *American Scientist*, May-June 1973.

Hynes, H.B.N., "The Stream and Its Valley." *International Association of Theoretical and Applied Limnology* (Stuttgart), 1975.

Jehl, Joseph R., Jr., "Far Flying Phalaropes." *National Geographic*, October 1981.

Johnson, William Oscar, "By the Shining Big Sea Water." *Audubon*, September 1979.

Kahl, M. Philip, "East Africa's Majestic Flamingos." *National Geographic*, February 1970.

"The Killer Weed Killer." *Discover*, January 1982.

Kohl, Larry, "Quebec's Northern Dynamo." *National Geographic*, March 1982.

LaBastille, Anne, "Acid Rain: How Great a Menace?" *National Geographic*, November 1981.

"Latin American Debtors Try to Form a United Front." *Time*, July 2, 1984.

Ledger, D. C., "The Velocity of the River Tweed and Its Tributaries." *Freshwater Biology*, 1981.

Leopold, Luna B., "Rivers." *American Scientist*, December 1962.

Leopold, Luna B., and W. B. Langbein, "River Meanders." *Scientific American*, June 1966.

Leopold, Luna B., and M. Gordon Wolman, "River Meanders." *Bulletin of the Geological Society of America*, June 1960.

Luoma, Jon R., "Troubled Skies, Troubled Waters." *Audubon*, November 1980.

McIntyre, Loren:
  "The Amazon." *National Geographic*, October 1972.
  "Brazil's Wild Frontier." *National Geographic*, November 1977.

May, Clifford D., "The Power and the Glory in Quebec." *GEO*, December 1979.

"The Mightiest Dam." *Fortune*, February 23, 1981.

el Moghraby, A. I., "A Study on Diapause of Zooplankton in a Tropical River — the Blue Nile." *Freshwater Biology*, 1977.

Nelson, Wilbur A., "Reelfoot: An Earthquake Lake." *National Geographic*, January 1924.

"Party für Einen Kontinent." *GEO*, March 1978.

Pillsbury, Arthur F., "The Salinity of Rivers." *Scientific American*, July 1981.

Powers, Charles F., and Andrew Robertson, "The Aging Great Lakes." *Scientific American*, November 1966.

Pryde, Philip R., "The 'Decade of the Environment' in the U.S.S.R." *Science*, April 15, 1983.

Ragotzkie, Robert A., "The Great Lakes Rediscovered." *American Scientist*, July-August 1974.

Ragotzkie, Robert A., and Gene E. Likens, "The Heat Balance of Two Antarctic Lakes." *Limnology and Oceanography*, 1964.

Regier, H. A., and W. L. Hartman, "Lake Erie's Fish Community: 150 Years of Cultural Stresses." *Science*, June 22, 1973.

Reisner, Marc, "Thirsty California." *GEO*, January 1981.

"Restoring Damaged Lakes." *Science*, February 1979.

Room, P. M., et al., "Successful Biological Control of the Floating Weed Salvinia." *Nature*, November 1981.

Rousmaniere, John, ed., "The Enduring Great Lakes." *Natural History*, August-September 1978.

Schmidt, Jeremy, "Into the Pumpkin." *Audubon*, September 1978.

Sheridan, David, "The Colorado: An Engineering Wonder without Enough Water." *Smithsonian*, February 1983.

Steinhart, Peter, "The City and the Inland Sea." *Audubon*, September 1980.

Steinhorn, Ilana, and Joel R. Gat, "The Dead Sea." *Scientific American*, October 1983.

Swain, Wayland R., "The World's Greatest Lakes." *Natural History*, August 1980.

Tinbergen, N., "The Curious Behavior of the Stickleback." *Scientific American*, December 1952.

Wintsch, Susan, "A Meander round New Harmony." *The Geographical Magazine*, June 1984.

Young, Gordon, "Mono Lake's Troubled Waters." *National Geographic*, October 1981.

Other Publications

"American Falls Dewatered 12 June, 1969." U.S. Army Corps of Engineers, Buffalo, 1969.

Britton, L. J., et al., eds., "An Introduction to the Processes, Problems, and Management of Urban Lakes." Circular 601-K, U.S. Geological Survey, U.S. Department of the Interior, no date.

Cairns, J., Jr., K. L. Dickson and E. E. Herricks, eds., *Recovery and Restoration of Damaged Ecosystems*. Proceedings of the International Symposium, Virginia Polytechnic Institute and State University, Blacksburg, Va., March 23-25, 1975. Charlottesville: University Press of Virginia, 1977.

"From Dream to Reality: The La Grande Complex — phase 1." Montreal: Société d'Énergie de la Baie James, no date.

Harper, Simon, transl., "Acidification Today and Tomorrow." A Swedish study prepared for the Stockholm Conference on the Acidification of the Environment. Stockholm: Ministry of Agriculture, Environment '82 Committee.

Moyle, Peter B., "Ecological Segregation among Three Species of Minnows (Cyprinidae) in a Minnesota Lake." Transactions of the National Fisheries Society, 1973.

"Preservation and Enhancement of The American Falls." International Joint Commission, Canada and United States, 1975.

Reighard, Jacob, "The Breeding Habits of the River Cub, *Nocomis Micropogon* (COPE)." Papers of the Michigan Academy of Science, Arts and Letters, 1942. Ann Arbor: The University of Michigan Press, 1943.

"Summary of Itaipu Project." Itaipu Binacional, December 1980.

"Welcome to the Imperial Irrigation District." El Centro, Calif.: Imperial Irrigation District, June 1982.

PICTURE CREDITS

Station. 67: © Terrence Moore. 68, 69: © 1980 Peter Menzel(3); © Terrence Moore. 71: © 1984 Ottmar Burwagen/Black Star. 72, 73: © 1981 Claus Meyer/ Black Star; Vieira de Queiroz/Camara Três/Black Star. 74, 75: © 1980 Claus Meyer/Black Star. 76, 77: © George Love/Kay Reese and Associates, Inc. 78: Heintges/ZEFA, Düsseldorf. 80: Ed Cooper. 81: Heinz Ambühl, EAWAG, Dübendorf. 83: Hans Pfletschinger, Archiv Toni Angermayer, Holzkirchen except third from top, © Stephen Dalton/NHPA, Ardingly, Sussex. 85: Biofotos, Farnham, Surrey — William H. Amos. 86: William H. Amos; Collection Varin-Visage/Jacana, Paris. 87: © William E. Ferguson — William H. Amos. 88, 89: © 1983 Patrice/Tom Stack and Associates — © Tom McHugh, Steinhart Aquarium/Photo Researchers. 91: Jim Brandenburg — Jeff Foott/Bruce Coleman Ltd., London. 93: © 1975 Dwight R. Kuhn. 94: Kim Taylor/Bruce Coleman Ltd., London. 95: Illustration by Greg Harlin of Stansbury, Ronsaville, Wood, Inc. 97: Biofotos, Farnham, Surrey. 98: Thomas E. Lovejoy. 99: © Loren A. McIntyre. 100, 101: Jane Burton/Bruce Coleman Ltd., London. 102, 103: R. Anton/Bruce Coleman Ltd., London. 102, 103: R. Andrew Odum/Peter Arnold, Inc.; Wolfgang Bayer/Bruce Coleman Ltd., London. 104: M. Woodbridge Williams, © 1962 National Geographic Society; © Loren A. McIntyre. 105: Marion and Tony Morrison, Woodbridge, Suffolk; © Loren A. McIntyre. 106, 107: Jane Burton/Bruce Coleman Ltd., London; Norman O. Tomalin/Bruce Coleman Inc. 108, 109: © Loren A. McIntyre; © Sven Lindblad/ Photo Researchers. 110, 111: Russ Kinne/Photo Researchers; Kenneth E. Lucas. 112: Michel Serraillier/Rapho, Paris. 115: Ed Cooper. 116: Illustrations by Greg Harlin of Stansbury, Ronsaville, Wood, Inc. 117: Peter Parks/Oxford Scientific Films, Oxford; G. I. Bernard/Oxford Scientific Films, Oxford; William H. Amos. 118-121: © David Doubilet. 122, 123: Hans Pfletschinger/Archiv Toni Angermayer, Holzkirchen. 124, 125: Wolfgang Steche/VISUM, Hamburg. 126: Nature, London — illustration by Greg Harlin of Stansbury, Ronsaville, Wood, Inc. — Nature, London. 130, 131: © Harald Sund. 132: Joseph R. Jehl Jr. 133: Wardene Weiser/ARDEA, London. 134, 135: Lee Lyon/Bruce Coleman Ltd., London. 136-141: Uwe George/GEO, Hamburg. 142, 143: L. H. Brown/ARDEA, London; Dr. Georg Gerster/Photo Researchers. 144: Ed Cooper. 146: Environmental Research Institute of Michigan. 148, 149: Museum of Comparative Zoology, Harvard University — © John Foster/Masterfile. 150, 151: Illustrations by Greg Harlin of Stansbury, Ronsaville, Wood, Inc. 152: James L. Amos, © National Geographic Society. 153: © 1973 News Group Chicago, Inc., reprinted with permission of the Chicago Sun-Times. 154: Michigan Sea Grant College Program. 155: Sea Lamprey Control Centre, Canada Department of Fisheries and Oceans; Tom Stack/Tom Stack and Associates. 157: Chart by Greg Harlin of Stansbury, Ronsaville, Wood, Inc. 158, 159: Map by Greg Harlin of Stansbury, Ronsaville, Wood, Inc. — © Wolfgang Kaehler. 160, 161: Guido Mangold, Munich — © Knut Hansen/Pitch, Paris. 163: Clyde H. Smith. 164: © 1982 Ted Spiegel/Black Star. 165: © 1982 Ted Spiegel/Black Star — chart by Greg Harlin of Stansbury, Ronsaville, Wood, Inc. 167: © Giorgio Lotti, Milan. 168: Punch, London. 169: © Terrence Spencer, London. 170, 171: Julian Calder, London.

INDEX

Time-Life Books Inc. offers a wide range of fine recordings, including a Rock 'n' Roll Era series. For subscription information, call 1-800-621-7026 or write Time-Life Music, P.O. Box C-32068, Richmond, Virginia 23261-2068.